TWENTIETH CENTURY INTERPRETATIONS
OF
CORIOLANUS

A Collection of Critical Essays

Edited by
JAMES E. PHILLIPS

Prentice-Hall, Inc. *Englewood Cliffs, N. J.*

A SPECTRUM BOOK

Contents

TWENTIETH CENTURY INTERPRETATIONS
OF

CORIOLANUS

Introduction

by James E. Phillips

I

William Shakespeare probably wrote *Coriolanus* in 1608 for production in that year by the King's Men, the theatrical company in which he was an actor, a major shareholder, and principal playwright. He was then 44 years old and at a significant point in his personal and professional development. The circumstances of his personal life—insofar as they can be determined—were at this time normal, even conventional, for a successful man of his years. His wife, Anne Hathaway, was apparently living with the younger daughter Judith in one of the best houses in Stratford, which Shakespeare seems to have visited on a commuting basis from London, and to which he would eventually retire. His elder daughter, Susanna, had made a good marriage to Dr. John Hall of Stratford in 1607, the year before *Coriolanus* was produced. His father, John Shakespeare, had died in 1601, two years before the first publication of *Hamlet*. More significant, perhaps—given the influence of Coriolanus's mother Volumnia on her son—is the fact that Shakespeare's own mother, Mary Arden, died in 1608, the year in which the play was presumably written.

At this same time Shakespeare was at the height of a professional career which had begun almost twenty years before, when one of his earliest plays, *The Third Part of King Henry the Sixth*, had brought from a rival playwright, Robert Greene, the envious taunt that this "upstart crow" considered himself to be "the only Shake-scene in a country." By 1598 a less prejudiced commentator, Francis Meres, had hailed Shakespeare as England's rival to Ovid for *Venus and Adonis*, *The Rape of Lucrece*, and the as-yet-unpublished "sugared sonnets." Meres had also praised Shakespeare as the equal of Plautus for comedy, citing among other plays *The Comedy of Errors*, *The Merchant of Venice*, and *A Midsummer Night's Dream*; and as the equal of Seneca for tragedy on the basis of such plays as *Titus Andronicus*, *Romeo and Juliet*, *Richard III*, and *Richard II*. Meres' accolade is all the more impressive when we recall that the major comedies and tragedies on which Shakespeare's reputation was ultimately to be based by contemporaries and by posterity were yet to come. Most of these latter appeared in the decade following 1598, ending with *Coriolanus*.

Coriolanus was not only Shakespeare's last tragedy, but it was also his last dramatization of Roman history, a subject that had attracted him throughout his career, from *Titus Andronicus* at the very outset, through *Julius Caesar* midway, to *Antony and Cleopatra,* written and produced in the year before *Coriolanus* appeared. Both as a tragedy and as a Roman play *Coriolanus* has, until recently, fared badly at the hands of critics and producers alike. Dr. Johnson could only say in its favor, somewhat cryptically, that it was "one of the most amusing of our author's performances." Coleridge admired the "wonderfully philosophic impartiality of Shakespeare's politics" in this play, but was nevertheless troubled by speeches like that of Aufidius in Act IV, although he expressed the hope that "becoming wiser I shall discover some profound excellence in that, in which I now appear to detect an imperfection." Reflecting this critical uneasiness about the play, theater people like Nahum Tate, Thomas Sheridan, and John Philip Kemble tried to adapt the work in productions intended to be meaningful to eighteenth- and nineteenth-century audiences. Among these, Kemble, with the help of the fabulous Sarah Siddons, apparently achieved an effect that was stunning if not Shakespeare's in a version which owed more to the poet James Thomson's rewriting of the play than it did to the original text.

Shortly before World War II, however, *Coriolanus*, in Shakespeare's own version as it is preserved in the Folio text of 1623, began to enjoy a remarkable success with audiences and critics alike. Productions in England, on the Continent, and in America have done well at the box office, notably those in Paris at the Comédie Française in 1934; in London at the Old Vic by Laurence Olivier in 1938 and by Richard Burton in 1954; and in New York's Central Park before massive, enthusiastic popular audiences in 1965. Meanwhile, as a relative flood of articles and books attest, critical opinion underwent a similar shift in favor of the play, perhaps reflecting or perhaps directing the corresponding shift in the tastes of producers and audiences.

It was quite possibly T. S. Eliot, in his remarkable *Coriolan* poems, who first recognized in Shakespeare's play the relevance to the twentieth century that accounts for this revival of interest in the work. In the second of these poems, "Difficulties of a Statesman," the hero is made to exclaim:

    O mother
    What shall I cry?

and the Citizens are made to respond:

We demand a committee, a representative committee of investigation
RESIGN RESIGN RESIGN[1]

Here, two basic themes of the play immediately meaningful to the
modern mind are brought sharply into focus. One is the psychological
dilemma created by a domineering mother, who in order to find vicarious gratification of her own subconscious ambitions forces her son into
a tragic choice. The other is the political dilemma of a brilliant military leader who is thus forced, against his own nature and tempera-
ment, into a position of governmental leadership for which he is hope-
lessly unqualified. Eliot's words direct us to the central issues that help
to explain the appeal of *Coriolanus* to twentieth-century critics and
audiences. Reversing his points for convenience of analytical discussion, they might be considered as, first, the political context within
which the personal tragedy of the hero is set; and second, the complex
psychological problem of the tragic hero himself.

II

Shakespeare's Roman plays, unlike *Hamlet, Othello, Lear,* and *Macbeth,* are invariably almost as much concerned with political issues as
they are with the personal tragedy of the heroes themselves. Indeed,
Julius Caesar, Antony and Cleopatra, and *Coriolanus* have, with some
justice, been called "political tragedies," and at least one recent critic
has called *Coriolanus* Shakespeare's "only great political play." [2]
Shakespeare's apparent preoccupation with political ideas and actions
in the Roman plays is probably explained by the fact that these works
are heavily dependent on Plutarch's *Lives of the Noble Grecians and
Romans* as source material, and Plutarch—especially in the translation
by Sir Thomas North which Shakespeare used—was primarily concerned with political morality. *Coriolanus,* of all the Roman plays, follows Plutarch most closely. For example, Menenius's celebrated "belly
speech" in I,i, a key passage in the design and development of the
whole play, is little more than a rendering in superb dramatic blank
verse of the speech as recorded in North's translation of Plutarch, as
well as in other English versions of the fable available to Shakespeare.[3]
The indebtedness to Plutarch perhaps explains in part why the personal tragedy of Coriolanus is presented in the fully developed political context which has become a focal point for much of the recent critical and popular reaction to the play.

[1] See this volume, p. 102.
[2] A. P. Rossiter, *"Coriolanus."* See this volume, p. 62.
[3] Cf. Hermann Heuer, "From Plutarch to Shakespeare: A Study of *Coriolanus,"
Shakespeare Survey,* X (1957), 54-55.

The twentieth-century response to *Coriolanus* in political terms is vigorous but sharply divided, attesting to the continuing vitality of this aspect of the work. The play has been both hailed and condemned as either propaganda for the totalitarian state or as a socialistic attack on the evils of dictatorship. For example, in the 1934 production at the Comédie Française, Paris police were called out to restrain demonstrators protesting against what they regarded as the antidemocratic sentiments of the play; two years later, in Pasadena, California, there were clear, if more restrained, complaints about a production of the play which was regarded locally as communistic because of its sympathetic representation of the rebellious common people of Rome. This and other provocative issues obviously embedded in the play—for example, the problem of the successful military hero who seeks to move into a position of political leadership—undoubtedly contribute to the continuing interest in *Coriolanus* as a political tragedy.[4]

The diverse readings of the political aspects of the play by twentieth-century critics and producers have led inevitably to speculation about Shakespeare's own political views as they are revealed in *Coriolanus*. Arguments have been advanced by various observers that he was a fascist, a republican, a democrat, a socialist, a communist. Most of such speculation is beside the dramatic point. If we take Menenius's "belly speech" and the imagery that it controls throughout the play as a guide to the political framework of the tragedy, it becomes evident that Shakespeare, with his customary detachment and objectivity, is simply concerned with making dramatic capital of the inevitable conflicts that exist, human nature being what it is, between the rulers and the ruled in what theoretically could be an ideal political society.

Menenius's so-called "belly speech" to the rebellious citizens in I,i, comparing the body politic to the body human, employs one of the many analogies used by Shakespeare and his contemporaries to describe this ideal society. Such analogies are based on the assumption that God created all things according to a single divine plan. It was argued that when one looks at the heavens, or the beehive, or the human body, or the body politic, one finds an identical corporate order in which each separate part, endowed with its own particular qualifications—its "vocation"—functions in its own appropriate place for the present welfare and the final purpose of the whole structure. Whether the structure be the stable heavens, a beehive intended by God to produce honey, a human body intended to be healthy, or a body politic intended to assure justice and prosperity for all, maintenance of order and degree based on vocation was regarded as essen-

[4] Cf. Rossiter, *"Coriolanus,"* this volume, p. 62; and A. A. Smirnov, *Shakespeare: A Marxist Interpretation,* this volume, p. 105.

tial to the fulfillment of the divine purpose for which each structure was created.

Shakespeare earlier had used such analogies to suggest, sometimes perhaps ironically, this ideal concept of corporate human society. In *Troilus and Cressida*, Ulysses combined two of these images in his effort to persuade the discordant Greek military society to conform to the ideal pattern of organization:

> When that the general is not like the hive
> To whom the foragers shall all repair,
> What honey is expected? Degree being vizarded,
> The unworthiest shows as fairly in the mask.
> The heavens themselves, the planets, and this centre
> Observe degree, priority, and place,
> Insisture, course, proportion, season, form,
> Office, and custom, in all line of order.   (I,iii)

Even earlier, in *Henry V*, the Archbishop of Canterbury had developed the same concept of social order in similar analogical terms:

> Therefore doth heaven divide
> The state of man in divers functions,
> Setting endeavor in continual motion,
> To which is fixed, as an aim or butt,
> Obedience; for so work the honey-bees,
> Creatures that by a rule in nature teach
> The act of order to a peopled kingdom.
> They have a king and officers of sorts,
> Where some, like magistrates, correct at home,
> Others, like merchants, venture trade abroad,
> Others, like soldiers, armed in their stings,
> Make boot upon the summer's velvet buds,
> Which pillage they with merry march bring home
> To the tent-royal of their emperor; . . .   (I,ii)

The concept of an ideal political society embodied in this imagery corresponds to that taken for granted by Menenius and his audience of rebellious citizens. In this confrontation the imagery of the dialogue shifts to another analogy common in the period, that of the human body and the body politic, but the basic point is the same. Even the Second Citizen accepts for the purposes of political argument the idea of a corporate hierarchy of vocational degrees when, agreeing with Menenius, he is willing to recognize

> The kingly-crowned head, the vigilant eye,
> The counsellor heart, the arm our soldier,

> Our steed the leg, the tongue our trumpeter,
> With other muniments and petty helps
> In this our fabric. . . .   (I,i)

Menenius's point, like that of Canterbury, Ulysses, and most of Shakespeare's contemporaries, is that when all parts function in their proper
place according to their unique qualifications, then the purposes for
which God created the total organism are fulfilled. As the Duke of
Exeter puts it in *Henry V*, in language closely paralleling that in
Coriolanus:

> While that the armed hand doth fight abroad,
> The advised head defends itself at home;
> For government, though high and low and lower,
> Put into parts, doth keep in one consent,
> Congreeing in a full and natural close,
> Like music.   (I,ii)

Shakespeare finds dramatic conflict and interest not in the fulfillment of such an idealized pattern of social order, but rather in the
human weaknesses which make its fulfillment a difficult and often a
hopeless task. Canterbury and Exeter, for example, use the pattern almost cynically to justify an action of foreign conquest by Henry V
that promises to save their own positions at home. In *Troilus and
Cressida* the impassioned actions of Achilles and Troilus completely
violate the grand ideal set forth by Ulysses and bring the action to an
end which Oscar James Campbell has called mocking and satiric.[5] Sim-
ilarly, the ideal political society prescribed by Menenius serves mainly
as a measure of dramatically interesting human inabilities to conform
to such a pattern. Neither the citizens, the "great toe of this assembly,"
as Menenius calls one of them at the end of his speech, nor Coriolanus
himself, "the arm our soldier," can keep their proper places and perform their proper functions in the ideal body politic. Shakespeare's
concern as a dramatist is with questions of why, in human terms, they
cannot. Both parties violate the prescribed pattern by seeking, in effect, to take over the governing functions naturally assigned to the
"head" of the body politic, the functions of political leadership. Both
are shown to be unqualified by nature to do so, and both, by attempting to do so, create a diseased body politic.

Menenius's speech in I,i thus sets the pattern for the imagery of a
diseased body that dominates the play as all parties violate the natural
order. As Caroline Spurgeon has pointed out, "The images arising out
of this central theme of the body and sickness are many, nearly one-

---

[5] *Shakespeare's Satire*. Cf. this volume, p. 25.

fifth of the whole." ⁶ To Coriolanus, the citizens are measles and scabs, rubbing the itch of their opinion (I,ii). To Menenius, Coriolanus is "a limb that has but a disease;/ Mortal, to cut it off; to cure it, easy" (III,i). To Aufidius, Coriolanus will pour war "Into the bowels of ungrateful Rome" (IV,v). The repetition of such imagery in the play, so persistent that Miss Spurgeon finds it "wearisome," emphasizes Shakespeare's interest in making dramatic capital of the inevitable difference between the ideally healthy body politic as described by Menenius, and the diseased body politic which the realities of human nature produce.

Menenius, as Derek Traversi has noted, may be futile in his efforts to make all parties conform to the ideal order, but he is not the Polonius-like fool that he has sometimes been called.⁷ Regularly he urges "On both sides more respect . . . Lest parties . . . sack great Rome with Romans" (III,i). He sees both sides, plebians and patricians alike, violating the natural body politic, and in his dismay he calls a plague on both their houses:

> I would they were in Tiber! What the vengeance!
> Could he not speak 'em fair?

Whether or not Shakespeare agreed with the political norm insisted upon by Menenius is really beside the point insofar as the dramatic values of the play are concerned, and so is any argument about his attitude toward the leaders and the led in a political society. Shakespeare's treatment of the citizens and of Coriolanus alike reveals the complete detachment of the complete dramatist who is concerned only with the human elements that account for these aberrations from a given political norm.

This detachment is evident in his portrayal of the citizens, secondary as their role in the drama may be compared to that of Coriolanus. When the citizens act according to their proper vocation in a healthy body politic as "Our steed the leg, the tongue our trumpeter," or even as the essential "great toe of this assembly," Shakespeare goes out of his way to arouse our sympathy for them. Nowhere is such manipulation of our response made clearer than in the scene where the citizens, dutifully willing to give their voices to the new Consul, are sarcastically asked by Coriolanus: "Well then, I pray, your price o' th' consulship?" Their answer is movingly simple: "The price is to ask it

⁶ *Shakespeare's Imagery* (Boston: Beacon Hill Press, 1958), p. 347. Cf. also G. Wilson Knight, "The Royal Occupation: an Essay on *Coriolanus,*" this volume, p. 15.
⁷ *Shakespeare: The Roman Plays,* this volume, p. 108.

kindly" (II,iii). Here, as Coriolanus is at his arrogant worst, the citizens are at their honest best.

When, however, they attempt to act outside their proper order and degree, the citizens are less sympathetically treated. To this end, Shakespeare alters his source in Plutarch to show the corn riots of Act I not as a quiet demonstration of passive resistance, but rather as a threat of violence aimed at overthrowing the established order. In portraying their efforts to exercise political authority and control, Shakespeare regularly characterizes them as unqualified by nature to assume the functions of the kingly-crowned head in the body politic because of their instability and unreliability. As one of the citizens himself rather touchingly admits when he explains why he and his fellows have been called a monstrous many-headed multitude: "If all our wits were to issue out of one skull, they would fly east, west, north, south, and their consent of one direct way should be at once to all the points o' th' compass" (II,iii). Coriolanus himself, more predictably, denounces them as "no surer, no,/ Than is the coal of fire upon the ice" (I,i). Even the usually conciliatory Menenius explodes against the political interference of "the voice of occupation and/ The breath of garlic eaters" when Rome is finally and fatally threatened (IV,vi).

These and similar passages assailing the citizens have been the basis for charges that Shakespeare in this play is antidemocratic, just as those passages sympathetic to the citizens have elicited the contradictory charges that he is socialistic. Both sets of charges are irrelevant to the drama, of course. Shakespeare is only interested in showing how and why the "great toe of this assembly" attempts to take over the authority assigned to the "kingly-crowned head" in the ideal body politic.

It is in this connection that the Tribunes—Sicinius and Brutus—become dramatically and thematically important. They are, in our terms, ward-heeler politicians who pragmatically take into account the realities of the situation, in contrast to Menenius, who thinks only in terms of the ideal. The Tribunes know that if Coriolanus is elected, their own power will be threatened: "Then our office may,/ During his power, go sleep" (II,i). They also know the political character of the citizens whom they represent, recognizing that same instability which the citizens themselves admit. As Sicinius says, "they/ Upon their ancient malice will forget/ With the least cause these his new honours" (II,i). And finally, they know the political weakness of their adversary, Coriolanus, whose "soaring insolence/ Shall touch the people" and "will be his fire/ To kindle their dry stubble; and their blaze/ Shall darken him for ever" (II,i). Operating on these pragmatic bases, the Tribunes are brilliantly effective in swaying the "many-headed multitude" to violate Menenius's ideal body politic and thereby contribute to its disease. By persuading the citizens to revoke their election of Coriolanus, the Tribunes reveal themselves at their demagogic best. Sicinius exhorts the plebians:

> Say you chose him
> More after our commandment than as guided
> By your own true affections, and that your minds,
> Pre-occupi'd with what you rather must do
> Than what you should, made you against the grain
> To voice him consul. Lay the fault on us. (II,iii)

Thus playing on the citizens' political instability, acknowledged by all parties, the Tribunes shrewdly manage to protect their own position in the establishment. Yet Shakespeare, with his usual dramatic objectivity, makes it clear that the Tribunes in their action are not totally wrong nor totally unconcerned with the general political good. As Brutus concludes, "This mutiny were better put in hazard/ Than stay, past doubt, for greater" (II,iii). He and Sicinius are fully aware of the raw political fact that Coriolanus, as the "arm our soldier," is no more qualified to assume the functions of the "kingly-crowned head" than is the "great toe of this assembly" whom they represent, and that, better sooner than later, the showdown must come.[8]

III

Shakespeare's interest as a dramatist centers on how Coriolanus violates the ideal body politic, and perhaps more importantly, on what impels him to do so. The basic questions are succinctly put by Aufidius when he speculates as to the reasons that made Coriolanus, against nature, seek to move "from the casque to the cushion"—that is, from the helmet, symbol of the battlefield, to the cushioned seat of political authority (IV,vii). Aufidius does not provide conclusive answers to the questions he raises, but his speculation serves to focus attention on one of the central dramatic concerns of the play—the influences that move a born soldier to seek a political authority which he is clearly not qualified to assume.

In the first act of the play Shakespeare carefully delineates the military brilliance and effectiveness of the hero. All parties acknowledge these qualities in Coriolanus. Even the rebellious First Citizen admits that he "could be content to give him good report for 't" (I,i). The soldier's personal valor and skill are demonstrated in action when he alone enters the gates of Corioli, and when, subsequently, he defeats Aufidius in hand-to-hand combat to secure a victory for Rome. As Paul Jorgensen perceptively observes, these actions reveal not the

[8] Cf. John Palmer, *Political Characters of Shakespeare,* this volume, p. 109.

military leader—his troops, after all, desert him—but rather, the heroic individual soldier.[9] As Shakespeare portrays him in this role,
Coriolanus seems almost endearingly modest and humble, albeit, as
one critic has observed, his is "the modesty of a god." Aware of his
proper vocation and function in the body politic, however, he well
deserves to feel proud of his accomplishments as the essential "arm
our soldier." As he himself says when honors are being heaped upon
him:

> I have done
> As you have done, that's what I can; induc'd
> As you have been, that's for my country.   (I,ix)

In this same first act, however, Shakespeare just as clearly points up
those traits and attitudes in Coriolanus which disqualify him as a potential political leader. He is certainly not portrayed as the "father of
his children" or the "shepherd of his flock," or as any of the other
symbols in Renaissance ideology for the kingly-crowned head. On the
contrary, he is distrustful and contemptuous of the common people
whom he will be asked to lead. To him, they are politically unstable
and untrustworthy; "Trust ye?" he shouts at them in his first speech in
the play; "With every minute you do change a mind,/ And call him
noble that was now your hate,/ Him vile that was your garland" (I,i).
This, of course, is ironically the same view of the citizens that they
take of themselves as "the many-headed multitude." But while prag-
matists like the Tribunes and even an idealist like Menenius know
how to deal coolly and expediently with such realities of politics,
Coriolanus can only react against them with violent frustration and
rage. He is revolted just as violently by the plebians for personal, even
physical, reasons. "Bid them wash their faces/ And keep their teeth
clean," he remarks as the citizens humbly approach to give him their
votes (II,iii); and in his final denunciation of them when he banishes
himself, he begins with an outburst of almost physiological revulsion:

> You common cry of curs! whose breath I hate
> As reek o' th' rotten fens, whose loves I prize
> As the dead carcasses of unburied men
> That do corrupt my air.   (III,iii)

In no respect, political or personal, is Coriolanus portrayed by Shakespeare as qualified to assume the functions of the "kingly-crowned
head" in the body politic as these functions were set forth in the Renaissance either by the idealistic followers of Erasmus's *Education of a*

---

[9] "Shakespeare's Coriolanus: Elizabethan Soldier," this volume, p. 109.

Christian Prince, or by the realistic followers of Niccolo Machiavelli's *The Prince*; or, for that matter, by anyone in any age wise in the ways of political leadership.

The central dramatic interest comes to focus, then, on the question explicitly put by Aufidius: Why does Coriolanus seek to move from the casque to the cushion? Shakespeare seems to go out of his way to make clear that personal ambition on the part of the hero is not a motivating factor in this fatal move. When, after his soldierly triumphs, his mother first hints that Coriolanus might move on to higher things, he disclaims any such political ambitions in a simple statement reflecting his basic agreement with the idea of a healthy body politic as described by Menenius. He says to her, "Know, good mother,/ I had rather be their servant in my way/ Than sway with them in theirs" (II,i). The statement is completely consistent with his earlier demurrer to the praises of Titus Lartius: "I have done/ As you have done, that's what I can; induc'd/ As you have been, that's for my country" (I,ix). Clearly, this is not a tragedy of personal, political ambition.

In the opening lines of the play, however, Shakespeare immediately directs attention to the force that will persuade Coriolanus to make his fatal decision to move from the casque to the cushion. That force is his mother, Volumnia. She had, in fact, impelled him to move to the casque in the first place. As the First Citizen observes when he comments on the military achievements of the hero, "Though soft-conscienc'd men can be content to say it was for his country, he did it to please his mother" (I,i). This observation is borne out by the careful attention which the dramatist thereafter gives to Volumnia's influence in the shaping of her son's military career from the very beginning. Shakespeare expands in some detail Plutarch's hint that Coriolanus was early left without a father, and that he lived with his mother even after his marriage. In the play, Volumnia boasts to her daughter-in-law Virgilia that she had sent her only son to the wars when he was "but tender-bodied" in the hope that his prowess would give her a kind of vicarious satisfaction; as she says, even if he had died, "his good report should have been my son; I therein should have found issue" (I,iii). The prospect of his "bloody brow," which shocks Virgilia almost into fainting, supremely delights the mother, who also—in the most brilliant symbolic image of the play—proudly regards the violent tearing apart of a butterfly by Coriolanus's young son as "One on's father's moods" (I,iii).

Freudian commentators have had much to say about the nature of the influence which this domineering mother exercises on her son. Summarizing their point of view, Norman Holland writes: "Coriolanus behaves in adult life (in the contrived world of the tragedy) like a man who, through early frustrations, developed an extraordinary amount of unmastered aggression which his mother diverted from herself onto other objects." [10] Whatever the clinical explanations may be, the dramatic facts as developed by Shakespeare make it clear that Coriolanus's fatal decision to move from the casque to the cushion, against his own nature and inclination, is determined by the influence of his mother. She is to him as the Tribunes are to the citizens in revealing the human elements that work to make the political ideal set forth by Menenius tragically impossible of attainment.

On two crucial occasions Shakespeare portrays dramatically the way in which Volumnia's influence operates. The first occurs in Act III when Coriolanus is urged by his friends among the Roman aristocracy to return to the citizens and seek to regain the vote of confidence which, under the politic direction of the Tribunes, they have just revoked. With complete self-awareness of his own lack of vocation, Coriolanus rejects the arguments of his friends that he stand again for the consulship. Then his mother is introduced to plead with him to return. Despite her appeals to his patriotism, to a political realism which she possesses but he does not, and to his filial duty, he resists. "I will not do 't," he exclaims, "Lest I surcease to honour mine own truth." At this point Volumnia plays what here and later will prove to be her trump card. "At thy choice, then," she says; "Come all to ruin! . . . for I mock death/ With as big heart as thou." Where every other appeal of friends and mother alike had failed, this suggestion that his action could possibly cause his mother's death immediately melts the resistance of the son. "Pray, be content./ Mother, I am going to the market-place;/ Chide me no more," he says, and goes off to the political disaster that leads to his banishment (III,ii).

Precisely the same pattern of psychological action and reaction is portrayed, even more extensively, in the final catastrophic action of the play (V,iii). Coriolanus, having joined with his old enemy Aufidius to bring Rome to its knees, is approached by delegations pleading with him to spare the city. As before, he spurns the appeals of old friends and associates, such as Cominius and Menenius. He remains silently adamant before the presence of his weeping wife and kneeling son. Even his mother's by-now-familiar arguments based on patriotism, family honor, and filial duty fail to move him. "He turns away," she exclaims. Finally, she again plays her trump card: "So we will home to Rome,/ And die among our neighbors." There follows one of the most celebrated moments of dramatic silence in Shakespeare when, according to the Folio stage direction, *"He holds*

[10] *Psychoanalysis and Shakespeare* (New York: McGraw-Hill, Inc., 1966), p. 328. Cf. also *ibid.*, pp. 157–62 for a judicious survey of recent psychoanalytical commentary on the play.

her by the hand, silent." [11] And once again, under the threat that
he will be committing matricide if he follows his own course,
Coriolanus yields to his mother, but this time with a helpless awareness of the tragic consequences for himself:

> O mother, mother!
> What have you done? . . .
> You have won a happy victory to Rome;
> But, for your son,—believe it, O believe it—,
> Most dangerously you have with him prevail'd,
> If not most mortal to him.

Aufidius is standing by to assure us, in an aside, that this capitulation
by Coriolanus to his mother will indeed be most mortal to him.

Shakespeare portrays the tragedy of Coriolanus as lying not so
much in this fatal political decision as in his belated recognition of
the maternal influence that has made him what he is and what he
is about to become. As Aufidius and the Volscians close in for the
kill in the last scene of the play, it is not fear of physical death
that overwhelms Coriolanus; "Cut me to pieces, Volsces," he cries;
"men and lads,/ Stain all your edges on me" (V,vi). Instead, it is a
psychological *coup de grace* shrewdly delivered by Aufidius that
reveals the real tragedy of this military hero. When Coriolanus,
charged with treason and cowardice by his arch-enemy, exclaims in
frantic disbelief, "Hear'st thou, Mars," Aufidius replies, "Name not
the god, thou boy of tears." In the ensuing passages of soldierly
defiance of his enemies Coriolanus constantly, and almost incoher-
ently, reverts to that word, "Boy." This is what has hurt. It is the
word that finally shocks him into a belated and tragic recognition
of the facts of his life. As his mother's "boy" he has been impelled
to move, against his own nature and inclination, from his successful
role as "the arm our soldier" to his ill-starred effort to assume the
functions of the kingly-crowned head.[12] Hence the tragic poignancy
—a quality usually denied Coriolanus by critics—of his celebrated
next-to-last utterance in the play:

> If you have writ your annals true, t'is there
> That, like an eagle in a dove-cote, I

[11] Cf. Harley Granville-Barker, "*Coriolanus:* Introduction," this volume, p. 37;
and Maurice Charney, "The Dramatic Use of Imagery in Shakespeare's *Coriolanus*," this volume, p. 74.

[12] Cf. C. K. Hofling, "An Interpretation of Shakespeare's *Coriolanus*," this volume, p. 84; and Rufus Putney, "Coriolanus and His Mother," this volume,
p. 104.

> Flutter'd your Volscians in Corioli;
> Alone I did it. "Boy!"   (V,vi)

Coriolanus, as most commentators agree, does not appear to be a tragic hero on the scale of Hamlet, Othello, Lear, or Macbeth. These struggle with inner conflicts and dilemmas throughout the action of their respective plays. Throughout the action of *Coriolanus* the hero is only dimly—perhaps only subconsciously—aware of his inner conflict and dilemma.[13] Outwardly, he remains arrogantly sure of himself and of the rightness of the course that his mother has imposed upon him. Then comes the final, awful moment of realization when the "boy" understands why the course of action which he, almost inevitably, has had to follow will be indeed most mortal to him. In this recognition, I think, lies the sudden tragic impact of the play. The prospering and secure "arm our soldier," having attempted to move from "the casque to the cushion" against his own nature and even his own will, comes to a full awareness, as do we, of those elements in human nature that make Menenius's ideal body politic so difficult, if not impossible, to realize. T. S. Eliot's lines, as suggested earlier, probably best summarize the essence of this political tragedy when they make Coriolanus implore, "Mother, what shall I cry," while the people demand—perhaps with a concern for Rome and for Coriolanus himself beyond their own comprehension—"Resign Resign Resign."

[13] Cf. Charney, "The Dramatic Use of Imagery in Shakespeare's *Coriolanus*," this volume, p. 74.

PART ONE

Interpretations

The Royal Occupation:
An Essay on *Coriolanus*

by G. Wilson Knight

. . . The play's style is bare. It holds little of the undulating, heaving swell of *Othello*'s music, the fireworks of *Julius Caesar,* the fine frenzies of *Lear* or *Macbeth*; it usually refuses the deeps of passion's threnody that toll the pilgrimage of *Timon.* Rather there is here a swift channeling, an eddying, twisting, and forthward-flowing stream; ice-cold, intellectual, cold as a mountain torrent and holding something of its iron taste. We are in a world of hard weapons, battle's clanging contacts, civic brawls about "grain" and "corn"; a town-life somewhat limited and provincial, varied with the sickening crashes of war. There is little brilliance, little colour. Some lovely natural images stand out, but they scarcely build any dominant delight till the last act, for which, however, they serve to prepare us. Here even fishes may have metallic fins:

> He that depends
> Upon your favours swims with fins of lead
> And hews down oak with rushes.   (i. i. 183)

The imagery is often metallic—such as "leaden pounds" (iii. i. 314), or "manacles" (i. ix. 57) or "leaden spoons, irons of a doit" (i. v. 5), or as when Coriolanus' harshness forces his mother to kneel "with no softer cushion than the flint" (v. iii. 53). This metal suggestion blends naturally elsewhere with the town setting. There is frequent mention of buildings. We hear of "hunger" breaking "stone walls" (i. i. 210), of "unroofing" the city (i. i. 222), of "the spire and top of praises" (i. ix. 24). There is reference to "Publius and Quintus"

"The Royal Occupation: An Essay on Coriolanus." *From* The Imperial Theme *by G. Wilson Knight (London: Methuen & Co., Ltd., 1951, 1954), pp. 155-65. Reprinted by permission of the publisher. The essay has been slightly abridged for this volume.*

who "our best water brought by conduits hither" (II. iii. 250). Antium
is praised for its fine buildings:

> A goodly city is this Antium. City,
> 'Tis I that made thy widows: many an heir
> Of these fair edifices 'fore my wars
> Have I heard groan and drop . . .   (IV. iv. 1)

—a grim boast. The plebeians short-sightedly have helped to "melt
the city leads" upon their own "pates" (IV. vi. 82), their "temples"
will be "burned in their cement" (IV. vi. 85). The fire-metal association is reflected rather differently in:

> One fire drives out one fire, one nail one nail.   (IV. vii. 54)

Such references often derive from the essentially "civic" setting.
And the present civilization is clearly a hard one—a matter of brick
and mortar, metals and stones. This is not the world of *Antony and
Cleopatra*. There human civilization catches a divine fire and blazes
back to the sun and moon something of their universal glory. Consider how Antony describes the rich ooze of Nile, sun-fecundated
and pregnant of harvest riches (*Antony and Cleopatra*, II. vii). Then
turn to *Coriolanus*:

> The Volsces have much corn; take these rats thither
> To gnaw their garners.   (I. i. 254)

We hear of "one poor grain or two" from "a pile of noisome musty
chaff" (v. i. 26–27). Here "store-houses" are "crammed with grain"
(I. i. 83), the belly is "the store-house and the shop" (I. i. 137) of the
body. "'Tis south the city mills" is a natural phrase (I. x. 31). The
difference from the wide universalism in *Antony and Cleopatra* is
vivid. We are limited by city walls. And cities are here metallic, our
world constricted, bound in by hard walls: and this constriction, this
suggestion of hardness, is rooted deep in our theme. The persons of
Antony and Cleopatra continually show a tendency to cohere, to
make friends with each other. Hostile cities are here ringed as with
the iron walls of war, inimical, deadly to each other, self-contained.
Thus our city imagery blends with war imagery, which is also "hard"
and metallic. And that itself is fused with the theme of Coriolanus'
iron-hearted pride. The whole association is bound closely in a speech
of Menenius, in which a building is emblematic of Coriolanus' hardness of soul in warring against his native town:

Menenius. See you yond coign o' the Capitol, yond corner-stone?
Sicinius. Why, what of that?
Menenius. If it be possible for you to displace it with your little finger,

there is some hope the ladies of Rome, especially his mother, may pre-
vail with him.   (v. iv. 1)

And even when the iron pride is vanquished, the ladies deserve "to
have a temple built them" (v. iii. 207).

War is here violent, metallic, impactuous. It does not exactly attain
the sunset glow of Othello's romance, his "pride, pomp, and circumstance of glorious war." Nor is it so grimly portentous and horror-
burdened as the warring of Macbeth and Banquo with the rebel
chiefs. Yet it is very much a thing of blood and harshness, and,
especially, metal. Coriolanus' wars are terrible in their ringing, iron
blows; in the breaking through city walls; in the clamorous con-
comitant of sounding "alarums." Weapons are scattered throughout
the play—they even invade the purely civic themes. Thus "wives
with splits and boys with stones" may rise against Coriolanus in
Antium (iv. iv. 5). Again,

> But make you ready your stiff bats and clubs:
> Rome and her rats are at the point of battle:
> The one side must have bale.   (i. i. 165)

The epithet "stiff" is as typical of this play as "soft" is of *Antony
and Cleopatra*. Coriolanus is "a rod" to Rome's friends (ii. iii. 99).
War is ever "hard" here. Thus the "casque" is contrasted with the
"cushion" (iv. vii. 43), and the same contrast appears in:

> When steel grows soft as is the parasite's silk
> Let him be made a coverture for the wars!   (i. ix. 45)

Again,

> . . . This peace is nothing, but to rust iron, increase
> tailors, and breed ballad-makers.   (iv. v. 233)

Numerous weapons—it is unnecessary to observe them in detail—are
mentioned throughout, as when we hear of soldiers "filling the air
with swords advanced and darts" (i. vi. 61), or of the patricians as
"the helms of the state" (i. i. 79). Individual combats are things of
sickening impact, force opposed to force, violent, hard, metallic.
Coriolanus' soldiers may bear against Aufidius "a shield as hard as
his" (i. vi. 80). Aufidius, thinking of Coriolanus, tells how he

> . . . thought to crush him in an equal force,
> True sword to sword . . .   (i. x. 14)

Coriolanus was "wont to thwack" Aufidius (iv. v. 188); he "scotched
him and notched him like a carbonado" (iv. v. 198). Such violent
suggestions are powerful in Aufidius' greeting to Coriolanus:

> Let me twine
> Mine arms about that body, where against
> My grained ash an hundred times hath broke,
> And scarr'd the moon with splinters: here I clip
> The anvil of my sword . . .   (IV. v. 112)

Notice the "moon" infinity-suggestion. We have here an infinite,
but harsh, warrior-strength. "Anvil" is suggestive: so, also, Coriolanus
would "forge" a name for himself from burning Rome (v. i. 14).
"What his breast forges, that his tongue must vent" (III. i. 258).
Aufidius dreams of violent contests with Coriolanus:

> We have been down together in my sleep,
> Unbuckling helms, fisting each other's throat,
> And waked half dead with nothing.   (IV. v. 130)

He hoped "once more to hew" Coriolanus' "target from his brawn"
(IV. v. 126). Menenius tells the citizens that the state will keep its
course

> . . . cracking ten thousand curbs
> Of more strong link asunder than can ever
> Appear in your impediment.   (I. i. 72)

The play starts with a crowd of citizens eager to avenge their wrongs
with "pikes" (I. i. 24); "trail your steel pikes" (V. vi. 152) is a fitting
conclusion.

These violent crashes of contest are things of blood. "Blood" is
emphasized. Volumnia, stern mother of a warrior son, loves to picture
Coriolanus painted in such glory:

> . . . his bloody brow
> With his mail'd hand then wiping, forth he goes . . .   (I. iii. 37)

Virgilia is terrified at the thought:

> His bloody brow! O Jupiter, no blood!

And Volumnia answers:

> Away, you fool! it more becomes a man
> Than gilt his trophy: the breasts of Hecuba,
> When she did suckle Hector, look'd not lovelier
> Than Hector's forehead when it spit forth blood
> At Grecian sword, contemning.   (I. iii. 42)

Notice the desecration of the idea of "birth" in this passage, comparable with *Macbeth*. Cominius, in the battle, sees Coriolanus thus
spattered with gore:

> Who's yonder,
> That does appear as he were flay'd? O gods!
> He has the stamp of Marcius; and I have
> Before-time seen him thus.   (I. vi. 21)

We have a warfare of crashing blows and spurting blood. Its violence is emphasized throughout. Here human ambition attains its height by splitting an opponent's body, the final signature of honour is the robe and reeking caparison of blood. Now all our imagery of clanging contest, iron blows, blood, ambition, and warrior honour —it is heavy throughout, and strikes a note of harshness peculiar to this play—centres on Coriolanus. He enters "cursing" (I. iv. 29), and "bleeding" (I. iv. 61). He is not lit with the blaze of chivalry that aureoles Antony: he is a man of iron, mail-fisted. I will next show the especial relevance of this quality to Coriolanus. Here he is in his bloody pride, and iron fortitude:

> . . . his sword, death's stamp,
> Where it did mark, it took; from face to foot
> He was a thing of blood, whose every motion
> Was timed with dying cries: alone he enter'd
> The mortal gate of the city, which he painted
> With shunless destiny: aidless came off,
> And with a sudden re-inforcement struck
> Corioli like a planet: now all 's his:
> When, by and by, the din of war gan pierce
> His ready sense; then straight his doubled spirit
> Re-quicken'd what in flesh was fatigate,
> And to the battle came he; where he did
> Run reeking o'er the lives of men, as if
> 'Twere a perpetual spoil: and till we call'd
> Both field and city ours, he never stood
> To ease his breast with panting.   (II. ii. 111)

Notice the metallic suggestion: the city "gate," "din" which "pierces" his sense, the fine hyperbole of Coriolanus "striking" the whole town with planetary impact. All this is blended with "blood"—he is "a thing of blood," "painting" Corioli with its people's blood, himself "reeking." There is, too, "death." His sword is "death's stamp," he runs over "the lives of men," and "dying cries" punctuate his advance. Iron, blood, death. There is something terrible in this description. He is indeed ruthless as death himself, a "shunless destiny." [1] This is our grim protagonist. So he charges through the

---

[1] Compare *Othello*, III. iii. 275:
> 'Tis destiny unshunnable, like death.

action like a steel-headed spear a-wing in the air of battle, destructive. So, at the end, we are not surprised to find him turning into a
blind mechanism of self-centred pride:

> . . . when he walks, he moves like an engine, and the ground shrinks
> before his treading: he is able to pierce a corslet with his eye; talks like
> a knell, and his hum is a battery.   (v. iv. 19)

This is the price of his excessive and exclusive virtue. Grim as he is
in his warring and pride, we must observe, too, his essential virtue.
He is a thing complete, a rounded perfection. We can no more blame
him for his ruthless valour than we blame the hurtling spear for
finding its mark. And yet Coriolanus has no mark: that is his tragedy.
Compact of nobility and strength, he pursues his course. But he is
too perfect a pure unit, an isolated force: no deep love of country
is his. His wars are not for Rome: they are an end in themselves.
Thus his renegade attack on Rome is no strange thing. His course
obeys no direction but its own: he is a power used in the service of
power. The spear turns out, in mid flight, to be a boomerang, and
hurtles back on the hand that loosed it. So he whirls like a planet in
the dark chaos of pride, pursuing his self-bound orbit: a blind
mechanic, metallic thing of pride and pride's destiny.

Throughout the play we are aware of his "grim looks" (i. iv. 58)
and, as Titus Lartius aptly phrases it:

> The thunder-like percussion of thy sounds.   (i. iv. 59)

That line is typical of a curious twist of style here. Continually we
find, in prose or poetry, a violent and startling polysyllable set amid
humble companions, often monosyllables. I quote a few to suggest
their quality: "Here is the steed, we the caparison" (i. ix. 12); "Make
good this ostentation and you shall" (i. vi. 86); "But now 'tis odds
beyond arithmetic" (iii. i. 245) ; "Like interrupted waters and o'erbear
. . ." (iii. i. 249); "That love the fundamental part of state" (iii.
i. 151); "For we are peremptory to dispatch" (iii. i. 286); "In peril
of precipitation" (iii. iii. 102). That last recalls another fine phrase:

> That the precipitation might down stretch
> Below the beam of sight.   (iii. ii. 4)

Often there are two such lines successive:

> Unseparable, shall within this hour,
> On a dissension of a doit, break out.   (iv. iv. 16)

or,

> This is a poor epitome of yours,
> Which by the interpretation of full time . . .   (v. iii. 68)

Sometimes we find two thunderous words in one line, as when the rabble is forgotten and a Coriolanus and Aufidius are left in single combat:

> In acclamations hyperbolical;   (i. ix. 51)

and,

> Than violentest contrariety;   (iv. vi. 73)

or,

> Murdering impossibility, to make
> What cannot be, slight work.   (v. iii. 61)

The name "Coriolanus" itself fits well and aptly into this pattern:

> To his surname Coriolanus 'longs more pride
> Than pity to our prayers;   (v. iii. 170)

And,

> Coriolanus in Corioli.   (v. v. 90)

In prose, there is a sprinkling of strange polysyllables outstanding from plainer speech: microcosm (ii. i. 69), conspectuities (ii. i. 71), empiricutic (ii. i. 128), cicatrices (ii. i. 163), carbonado (iv. v. 199), directitude (iv. v. 221), factionary (v. ii. 29). Many of these cause blank amazement among the rabble, or Volscian menials: and are thus related to the main idea of the aristocrat contrasted with commoners. So, in our line units, there is, as it were, an aristocrat among a crowd of plebeian words, and often that protagonist word falls with a hammer-blow that again reminds us of metal:

> 'Tis fond to wail inevitable strokes.   (iv. i. 26)

Again, with implicit reference to "harshness," there is the clanging note of:

> A name unmusical to the Volscians' ears
> And harsh in sound to thine.   (iv. v. 64)

Such protagonist words apply aptly to our protagonist's actions:

> That would depopulate the city, and
> Be every man himself.   (iii. i. 264)

and,

> . . . to wind
> Yourself into a power tyrannical.   (III. iii. 64)

But, whether directly or indirectly related to Coriolanus, each anvil-blow of such lines as these reminds us of "the thunder-like percussion of his sounds"; and each seems to strike another rivet in his iron armoury of pride. Each line reflects the whole play, where Coriolanus strides gigantic, thunderously reverberating his aristocracy above the multitude.

Nature-images point us to the same thought. They both contrast with our metallic images, preparing us for the love-victory later, and point the natural excellence of our hero. He is rather like a finely-modelled motor-cycle, flashing in bright paint and steel, every line suggesting power and speed, standing among a row of drab pedal-bicycles. Thus there is continual contrast between strong and weak things in nature, usually animals, which contrast is directly or indirectly related to the Coriolanus-plebeian opposition. Animals, and other nature references, go in pairs. We have lions and hares, foxes and geese (I. i. 175–6); oaks and rushes (I. i. 185); a bear scattering children (I. iii. 34); a boy and a butterfly (I. iii. 63–71); men and geese (I. iv. 34) ; the cat and the mouse (I. vi. 44); a hare being hunted (I. viii. 7); weeds before a vessel's keel (II. ii. 109); eagles and crows (III. i. 139); boys and butterflies again, butchers and flies (IV. vi. 94–95); Hercules shaking down ripe fruit (IV. vi. 99); a "harvest-man" mowing corn (I. iii. 39); the shepherd and the wolf (IV. vi. 110) . Such imagery continually suggests the inborn inequality of men. Coriolanus is endued from birth with nature's aristocracy. He exceeds Romans and Volscians alike—scattering his enemies like leaves before a wind, despising his own countrymen like vermin. Aufidius, indeed, is a "lion" he is "proud to hunt" (I. i. 239); but to him the Roman citizens are "camels" or "mules" (II. i. 270, 266), or "dogs" to be beaten for barking (II. iii. 224), their tribune an "old goat" (III. i. 177). The Volscians are suggested to be no better:

> . . . when they shall see, sir, his crest up again, and the man in blood,
> they will out of their burrows, like conies after rain, and revel all with
> him.   (IV. v. 223)

Such phraseology continually points us to a certain essential triviality in those who make up the crowds of Romans or Volscians. The Roman plebeians are as "a beast with many heads" which "butts" Coriolanus from Rome (IV. i. 1) . He is of a different stock from such animals. Even the patricians feel his inborn superiority:

> . . . the nobles bended
> As to Jove's statue, and the commons made
> A shower and thunder with their caps and shouts.
>
> (II. i. 281)

"Jove," and "thunder": Coriolanus is often imaged grim as a wrathful God. Elsewhere his "thunder" is contrasted with the "tabor" (I. vi. 25). He fights "dragon-like" (IV. vii. 23). Again:

> *Sicinius.* Is't possible that so short a time can alter the condition of a man?
> *Menenius.* There is differency between a grub and a butterfly; yet your butterfly was a grub. This Marcius is grown from man to dragon: he has wings; he's more than a creeping thing.   (v. iv. 9)

Again a vivid contrast, this time between Coriolanus superficially at least as a man among men and Coriolanus that ogre of self-nursed anger and unrelenting iron into which he develops. But his ugliness is ever but an excessive, because self-limited, beauty: the beauty of natural excellence, unbending to any law but his own. He is born into a sovereignty of strength and conscious superiority:

> I think he'll be to Rome
> As is the osprey to the fish, who takes it
> By sovereignty of nature.   (IV. vii. 33)

The same contrast rings out in his final boast:

> If you have writ your annals true, 'tis there,
> That, like an eagle in a dove-cote, I
> Flutter'd your Volscians in Corioli:
> Alone I did it.   (v. v. 114)

Yet a mightier power beats down his pride. At the climax love disarms his vengeance. When Volumnia pits his filial love against his pride, this new antagonism again finds noble expression in natural—or rather universal—imagery more powerful than that already observed. To Coriolanus, "the rock, the oak not to be wind-shaken" (v. ii. 118), his mother comes, strong in her weakness, comes to the iron giant of her own moulding:

> My mother bows;
> As if Olympus to a mole hill should
> In supplication nod.   (v. iii. 29)

Now it is he who is weak as a "gosling" (v. iii. 35). His mother kneels:

What is this?
Your knees to me? to your corrected son?
Then let the pebbles on the hungry beach
Fillip the stars; then let the mutinous winds
Strike the proud cedars 'gainst the fiery sun;
Murdering impossibility, to make
What cannot be, slight work.   (v. iii. 56)

Here, then, we have our Coriolanus-idea: something of iron strength
and natural excellence which sticks

. . . i' the wars
Like a great sea-mark, standing every flaw,
And saving those that eye thee!   (v. iii. 73)

But great as is this contrast, there is a greater. The simple power of
love is endued with a dignity and universal sanction comparable
only with "Olympus," the "stars," the "fiery sun." In that comparison
men and lions and all brave beasts are levelled with "molehills," and
"pebbles." Thus our style and imagery, whether of metals, of protagonist words, or of natural reference, point clearly the direction of
our analysis. . . .

Shakespeare's Satire: *Coriolanus*

by Oscar James Campbell

In *Coriolanus* we have Shakespeare's second and more successful experiment in tragical satire. The structure which in *Timon of Athens* was bare and almost crude has here become a suitable form in which to cast the Roman aristocrat's story. Yet the construction of this last of Shakespeare's tragedies has been almost universally deplored. Critics, realizing that its pattern is very different from the one which the poet employed in his great tragedies, have agreed to brand it as inept. A. C. Bradley, for example, believes that the author's unintentional departure from his usual practice accounts for the failure of the play to produce a sound tragic effect.[1] This usually acute critic did not allow for the fact that Shakespeare, at this time a thoroughly experienced dramatist, might have deliberately experimented with new dramatic structures.

It is natural enough to judge *Coriolanus* by the standards of conventional tragedy; in the first Folio it is entitled *The Tragedy of Coriolanus*. Bernard Shaw was one of the first to see that the play was not a tragedy at all. He solves the problem of *Coriolanus* by propounding a witty paradox. "It is," he asserts, "the greatest of Shakespeare's comedies." This perverse statement suggests the proper approach to the play. Shakespeare did not attempt to give *Coriolanus* the structure of a conventional tragedy. Neither in his presentation of the central figure nor in his construction of the plot does he follow orthodox tragic principles. Instead of enlisting our sympathy for Coriolanus, he deliberately alienates it. Indeed he makes the figure

[1] A. C. Bradley, "Coriolanus. Second Annual Shakespeare Lecture" (1 July, 1912), Proceedings of the British Academy 1911–12, pp. 457–73. Hazelton Spencer, in *The Art and Life of William Shakespeare* (1940), 346–50, takes a similar view. "In *Coriolanus*," says the critic, "he [Shakespeare] frankly takes the line of least resistance." The idea is that he simply followed mechanically the facts laid down in his source—"that is all."

partly an object of scorn. Instead of ennobling Coriolanus through
his fall and death, he mocks and ridicules him to the end. In brief,
he fills the trgedy so full of the spirit of derision that the play can
be understood only if it be recognized as perhaps the most successful
of Shakespeare's satiric plays. . . .

. . . *Coriolanus,* like all Shakespeare's other history plays, em-
bodies some of the author's political ideas. Some critics, to be sure,
hesitate to attribute any definite political views to him. The idolators
of the early nineteenth century and their modern representatives are
responsible for this transcendental attitude toward their hero. Shakespeare, they proudly assert, was not of an age, but of all time. Of all
movements in a given era, political squabbles are the most ephemeral.
Therefore to the idolators an assertion that Shakespeare expressed positive political opinions even in his chronicle history plays was the
rankest heresy. A. C. Bradley expressed their view when he wrote,
"I think it extremely hazardous to ascribe to him [Shakespeare] any
political feeling at all and ridiculous to pretend to any certainty on
the subject.[2] This betrays a strange view of the dramatist's art.
He, less than any other man of letters, dares to retire to an ivory tower,
remote from the social interests of his contemporaries, in order to
allow the trade winds from eternity to blow through his philosophic
mind. Shakespeare based his profound studies of human motive and
human passion upon a realistic appraisal of the various milieux in
which his characters came to life; and of all the environments in which
human beings must live, the political organization most interested
Shakespeare and his contemporaries. The problems of Tudor politics
obsessed them.

The usual view is that in *Coriolanus* Shakespeare expresses his
contempt for the common man and his conviction that political
power in the hands of the mob always brings disaster to the state.[3]
More recently critics have looked at the other side of the picture
and discerned in Coriolanus' conduct an exposure of the brutal
methods that dictators in every age must employ to retain their
absolute power.[4] Each of these apparently contradictory views is
partly correct. Though Shakespeare is not in this play showing his

[2] Bradley, *op. cit.,* p. 461.

[3] George Brandes, for example, in a chapter in *William Shakespeare, a critical
Study* (New York, 1902), emphasizes the absence in *Coriolanus* of "any humane
consideration for the oppressed condition of the poor" and his "physical aversion
for the atmosphere of the people." M. W. MacCallum expresses the more measured
view by admitting that "Shakespeare invariably treats crowds of citizens, whether
in the ancient or modern world . . . as stupid, disunited, fickle" (*Shakespeare's
Roman Plays and Their Background,* London, 1910, p. 470).

[4] Serge Dinamov, *Works of Shakespeare,* 4 vols., 1, xix.

contempt for the common man, he is nevertheless expressing his vigorous disapproval of democracy. In common with all political theorists of his age, he regarded it as the absence of all government— a form of organized disorder.[5]

But he does not lay all the blame for the social chaos on the plebs and its leaders. To his mind Coriolanus is equally guilty. He is a bad ruler. In the many volumes that the fifteenth and sixteenth centuries devoted to the education of a prince, the supreme magistrate —usually the king—is admonished to regard his subjects as his children and to be a father to them. He must sympathize with their trials and dangers and feel keenly his responsibility for their welfare. He must follow the example set by Henry V toward his soldiers in Shakespeare's play of that name. But Coriolanus acts in a manner diametrically opposed. He hates the people. On almost every occasion in which he meets them face to face he berates them and curses them vilely. Inevitably he finds them hostile and recalcitrant to his leadership—brave and efficient though it be in battle. Instead of correcting their faults, he goads them to anarchy by his hostility and violence. Coriolanus is thus as much responsible as the plebs for the political débâcle.

As a political *exemplum* the play presents a case of violent political disorder and reveals its causes. The trouble lies in the fact that no civil group performs its prescribed duties properly. As a result the divinely revealed pattern for the state is disrupted and society reels toward primal chaos. This lesson could not be clearly taught in the terms of tragedy. With its interest concentrated upon the tragic career of Coriolanus the man, an audience might easily ignore the political significance of the play. But the satiric form gave Shakespeare an opportunity to treat derisively both the crowd and Coriolanus, between whose "endless jars" the commonweal was sorely wounded. A careful analysis of the play will show how skillfully the political teaching, the central theme of every Elizabethan history play, has been fitted to the satiric form of the drama.

The play opens with a picture of a mutinous mob, in this way establishing immediately the atmosphere of social turmoil which is to exercise its destructive power throughout the action and to form a natural milieu for the subversive forces in the little world of Coriolanus' passions. In the midst of the uproar Menenius appears. He is the chief of the many commentators and expositors in this play who serve as Shakespeare's mouthpiece. He performs this service

---

[5] These ideas have been thoroughly presented in James E. Phillips, Jr.'s *The State in Shakespeare's Greek and Roman Plays* (N. Y., 1940), *passim.*

with a fussy garrulity that is intended to rouse our laughter. Later
in the play he explains that he is "a humorous [i.e., crotchety]
patrician and one that loves a cup of hot wine with not a drop
of allaying Tiber in't. . . . One that converses more with the but-
tock of the night than with the forehead of the morning. What I
think, I utter, and spend my malice in my breath" (II. i. 51–8 *passim*).
The character of this speech, particularly its unsavory metaphors,
stamps Menenius as Shakespeare's variant of the now familiar buffoon-
ish commentator. Like Carlo Buffone he says right things in the wrong
way, thus giving to his comments a kind of outrageous pertinence.

His first speech to the crowd only partly reveals these characteristics.
In order to persuade it to cease its revolutionary uproar, he tells the
fable of the rebellion which the other members of the body once
raised against the belly,

> That only like a gulf it did remain
> I' the midst o' th' body, idle and unactive,
> Still cupboarding the viand, never bearing
> Like labor with the rest.   (I. i. 101–4)

But the belly replies that by sending rivers of blood to all parts of
the body it serves as the source of the health and the very life of
the whole organism. The belly, it appears, stands in this parable for
the senators, and for Coriolanus in particular, because in Rome he
and his fellow patricians exercised the functions of the king. The
mutinous members of the body represent the plebeians.

The audience would have regarded this figure of the belly and its
functions as a speech designed to characterize Menenius—to stamp
him as a garrulous old man. But they would also recognize it as a
conventional way of stating a familiar principle of current political
philosophy. It would seem like a page torn from almost any political
primer. Because both the plebs and Coriolanus disregard the principles illustrated in Menenius' parable they bring disaster to Rome
and to themselves. The people, in seeking to exercise the functions of
a ruler, were permitting "the foot to partake in point of preëminence
with the head." They were instituting a form of democracy which
was universally regarded as a monstrous body of many heads.[5]
Coriolanus himself employs this figure to describe the proletariat.
As he stands outside the gate of Rome, whence he has been driven
by the mob, he exclaims

> The beast
> With many heads butts me away.   (IV. i. 2–3)

Elsewhere in the play he calls the plebs Hydra.[6] Through the repeated use of such familiar figurative language the author impressed his historical lesson upon his audience. No member of it could fail to recognize the drama as an exhibition of the forces of democracy at their destructive work. The most obvious lesson that the drama is designed to teach is, then, as follows: The people should never be allowed to exercise any of the functions proper to a ruler. That way lies anarchy. But the career of Coriolanus is to constitute an equally impressive warning: No ruler must act as cruelly and brutally toward his subjects as does this man. He is more of a slave driver than a kind father. Such a magistrate is always an architect of social confusion.

A character cast to play such an admonitory role cannot be treated like an ordinary tragic hero. And Shakespeare deals with Coriolanus from the moment of his first appearance through the whole course of the play to the catastrophe in a manner directly opposite to the one he invariably adopted for his real tragic protagonists. In the first place he endows all his true tragic heroes with many noble traits which appear and reappear through the play. In particular he puts into the mouths of other characters words of praise for the hero as they knew him before he became a slave to one of the subversive passions. Shakespeare also puts into his hero's mouth reflective soliloquies which reveal his struggles between good and evil, and win our sympathetic understanding even while he is losing his battle with destiny. Then, as his protagonist stands at the very brink of the catastrophe, the poet allows him to utter a poignant speech which recalls to the minds of the spectators the loftiness of his nature before he had been caught in the net of his tragic fate. Finally, after the hero's death some character who has survived the holocaust is likely to utter a brief encomium or a benediction upon the soul of the dead man. . . .

Coriolanus is treated in a completely different fashion. The very first comments made upon him are derogatory. The two citizens who discuss him in the opening scene are detractors. The first of them asserts that Coriolanus has served his country not from patriotic motives but only to please his mother and to flatter his own pride. The second feebly defends Coriolanus by saying, "What he cannot help in his nature, you account a vice in him." The first citizen, un-

---

[6] William Fulbecke in his *Pandectes of the Law of Nations* (1602) cites the history of Coriolanus to confirm his contention that the people is the "beast with many heads." This example he offers as part of his evidence drawn from history to prove that democracy is contrary to natural law.

impressed by the notion that innate faults are not vices, replies, "He hath faults (with surplus) to tire in repetition." This very first expository scene presents Coriolanus' passion nakedly, stripped of all nobility. It is what Mark Van Doren calls "an animal pride—graceless, sodden, and hateful." This initial exposition is but the first of many conversations about Coriolanus, all contributing features to a disagreeable portrait.

The accumulation of derogatory comment does much to set the satiric tone of the play. "Groups of people," says Mark Van Doren, "tribunes, citizens, servants, officers laying cushions in the Capitol, travellers on the highway, the ladies of his household—are forever exchanging opinions on the subject of Coriolanus. And the individuals who share with him the bulk of our attention are here for no other purpose than to make leading remarks about him." [7] In other words the play is crowded with satiric commentators.

When two or three characters gather together, the subject of their conversation is always Coriolanus. And even his wife's friend Valeria and his mother Volumnia, in contriving what they think is praise of Coriolanus, reveal the savage results of his pride. Valeria's description of the little boy at play becomes a revelation of his father's heady violence. She says, "I saw him [the boy] run after a gilded butterfly; and when he caught it, he let it go again and after it again, and over and over he comes and up again; catch'd it again; or whether his fall enrag'd him or how 'twas, he so set his teeth and tear it! O, I warrant, how he mammock'd it [tore it to shreds]" (I. iii. 66–71). Volumnia's comment on this incident—made with complete satisfaction—is "One on's father's moods." And she is right. Irascibility and anger are the emotions which Coriolanus most often displays—and properly, for they are the inevitable results of thwarted pride.

Of all the commentators Menenius is the least obvious in his hostility. That is because, being a buffoon, he inevitably draws the fire of some of the derision. Yet in his characterization of the tribunes, his unsavory metaphors arouse laughter, even while they furiously mock. Witness his vulgar description of the tribunes' attempt to act as judges: "When you are hearing a matter between party and party, if you chance to be pinch'd with the colic, you make faces like mummers, set up the bloody flag against all patience, and, in roaring for a chamber pot, dismiss the controversy bleeding, the more entangled by your hearing. . . . When you speak best unto the purpose, it is not worth the wagging of your beards; and your beards deserve not so honorable a grave as to stuff a botcher's cushion or to be entombed in an ass's packsaddle" (II. i. 81–7, 95–9). This is the buffoon at his expert best.

[7] Mark Van Doren, *Shakespeare,* New York, 1939, p. 10.

When this "perfect giber for the table" (and "giber" is an almost
exact equivalent for our slang "wise-cracker") turns his wit upon
Coriolanus, he realizes that it must combine exposition of the man's
nature with his ridicule. Once while attempting to excuse his friend's
violence, he says:

> His nature is too noble for the world,
> He would not flatter Neptune for his trident
> Or Jove for's power to thunder. His heart's his mouth;
> What his breast forges, that his tongue must vent
> And being angry does forget that ever
> He heard the name of death.   (III. i. 255–9)

The first line of his speech, torn from its context, has been used by
many critics to prove that Coriolanus' pride is the tragic flaw in an
otherwise noble nature.[8] But Menenius is speaking not of pride, but
of headlong anger. Even if the old patrician had meant to say that
the pride of Coriolanus was the infirmity of his noble mind, no one
in an Elizabethan audience would have mistaken his opinion for
Shakespeare's. By the third act even the slowest-minded spectator
would have recognized Menenius as a sort of buffoon and his comments as food for laughter.

After this attempt to palliate his hero's anger, Menenius returns to
his more characteristic vein of comment. Such is the tone of his description of his friend's appearance when rejecting the old man's appeal to save Rome: "He no more remembers his mother now than
an eight-year-old horse. The tartness of his face sours ripe grapes.
When he walks, he moves like an engine, and the ground shrinks
before his treading. He is able to pierce a corslet with his eye, talk
like a knell and his hum is a battery . . . He wants nothing of a god
but eternity and a heaven to throne in" (v. iv. 14–26 *passim*). This
is bitterly derisive comment, utterly inappropriate for a tragic hero
on the verge of his catastrophe, but just the sort of talk best calcu-
lated to keep alert to the end of the play the satiric attitude of an
unsympathetic audience.

This purpose is accomplished throughout the drama in still more
direct ways. Instead of revealing a rich inner nature in profound
poetic soliloquies, Coriolanus exhibits over and over again his one

---

[8] John W. Draper in an article called "Shakespeare's *Coriolanus:* A Study in
Renaissance Psychology," West Virginia Bulletin (Philological Studies III Sept.
1939, pp. 22–36) develops these ideas. He believes that *Coriolanus* is a perfect
illustration of the notions on this subject developed in Plutarch's *Morals*, La
Primaudaye's *The French Academie*, and Thomas Adams' *Diseases of the Soul*
(1616) first introduced into Shakespeare studies by Lily B. Campbell in her *Shakespeare's Tragic Heroes* (Cambridge, 1930).

ruling passion—the choler which Renaissance philosophers regarded
as the inevitable result of wounded pride. At every one of his encoun-
ters with the people his rage boils at their impertinence. His contempt
he displays through the insults which a "lonely dragon" or Caliban
might pour upon "rank-scented" men. When his soldiers retreat before the attack of the Volscians, he shouts:

> All the contagion of the South light on you,
> You shames of Rome! you herd of—. Biles and plagues
> Plaster you o'er, that you may be abhorr'd
> Farther than seen, and one infect another
> Against the wind a mile! You souls of geese
> That bear the shapes of men, how have you run
> From slaves that apes would beat!   (I. iv. 30–36)

For this voice we can feel only aversion. Yet its vigor and its lean
thrust form an almost perfect expression of the spirit of Juvenalian
satire. Indeed the bare poetic style of this play, lamented by most
critics, is exquisitely adapted to the author's derisive intentions.

Understanding the easy inflammability of Coriolanus, the tribunes
are able to teach the plebs just how to induce his paroxysms of anger.
When thus beside himself, he becomes their easy victim: "Put him to
choler straight," they advise,

> . . . Being once chafed, he cannot
> Be reined again to temperance; then he speaks
> What's in his heart; and that is there which looks
> With us to break his neck.   (III. iii. 25–30)

By following these instructions the mob produces a rhythmical re-
currence of Coriolanus' grotesque rage; and this stimulated repetition
of a vice or a folly is of the very essence of satire of every sort. It turns
Coriolanus into a jack-in-the-box. Every time his self-esteem is de-
pressed, it springs back with the same choler-distorted face. This emotional automatism deprives his pride and his anger of all dignity. It
makes him a natural object of derision.

Coriolanus is also his mother's puppet. Volumnia transforms him
into a terrified little boy every time the two confront each other.
Shakespeare may have intended her to represent an austere patrician
woman of early Rome, a worthy mother of grim warriors. Yet she
wins from her son not the respect of a man, but the frightened obedience of a whimpering urchin. His attitude toward her remains completely infantile.

It is Volumnia who has forced her son to become a soldier and to
exult in the blood and sweat of war. Plutarch describes Coriolanus as
driven to battle by an irresistible impulse of his own nature. But

Shakespeare tells us that it was Volumnia, "poor hen, who clucked him to the wars and home." This barn-yard figure incidentally deprives the martial impulses of Coriolanus of every shred of dignity. As a soldier he was and remains his mother's creature. Her proud boast is the truth:

> Thy valiantness was mine, thou suck'st it from me.
> (III. ii. 129)

When he is at the front, she relieves her anxiety by imagining him wading in triumph through seas of carnage and blood.

Though Volumnia has also bred into her son his contempt for the people, she knows that he must placate them. She realizes that if he is ever to become consul, he must stand in the market place and humbly beg for their votes. So at first she entreats him to go through the distasteful ceremony merely to please her:

> I prithee now, sweet son, as thou hast said
> My praises made thee first a soldier, so,
> To have my praise for this, perform a part
> Thou hast not done before.   (III. ii. 107–10)

But even for his mother's sake Coriolanus refuses to let his disposition be possessed by "some harlot's spirit," to turn his voice "into a pipe small as an eunuch," or to allow a "beggar's tongue make motion through his lips." His answer to her courteous pleading is a flat, "I will not do't."

Then Volumnia loses her temper and soundly scolds her son. Her burst of scorn and anger immediately brings him around, reducing him to the stature of a frightened child, ridiculously eager to pacify an irate parent:

> Pray be content [he almost whimpers];
> Mother, I am going to the market place;
> Chide me no more.
> . . . Look I am going.   (III. ii. 130–32; 134)

The contrast between his arrogant attitude toward all other persons in the drama and his infantile cowering before his mother's severity is ridiculous, and is intended to be so.

His last scene with Volumnia, in which she finally dissuades him from leading the victorious Volscians into Rome, is a kind of incremental repetition of the interview just described. When neither her pathetic appeals, made as she kneels before him, nor his wife's tears divert him from his purpose, his mother again loses her temper. She rises from her knees, crying

> Come, let us go.
> This fellow had a Volscian to his mother;
> His wife is in Corioles, and his child,
> Like him by chance. Yet give us our dispatch.
> I am hushed until our city be afire.
> And then I'll speak a little.   (v. iii. 177–82)

The old woman's fierce indignation again cows her son. Terrified by her anger, he cries out, like a helpless little boy:

> O mother, mother!
> What have you done? . . .

> O my mother, mother! O!
> You have won a happy victory to Rome;
> But for your son—believe it, O, believe it!—
> Most dangerously you have with him prevail'd.
>   (v. iii. 182–3; 185–8)

This repeated quailing before his mother deprives Coriolanus of the dignity every tragic hero must possess. He never submits to her will through conviction or a sense of duty. His surrender is never evidence of filial respect. It is always a boy's frightened submission to a domineering woman. His undeviating arrogance toward the rest of humanity thus seems to be not exaggerated self-esteem, but compensation for the fear of his mother. He never attains the mean between these two unnatural extremes of emotion, but careens wildly between them. This instability renders him at once absurd and doomed. The forebodings which seize him after his final yielding to his mother are fulfilled. They set him in the path which leads straight to his downfall.

When Coriolanus returns to the Volscian army, he finds Aufidius hostile. He has all along been jealous of the renegade Roman and now sees a chance to destroy him. Knowing how easy it is to drive Coriolanus into a fit of blind rage, he sets the stage for the undoing of his enemy in a scene which constitutes the finale of the drama. And a masterful scene it is—an admirable catastrophe for a satirically conceived tragedy. It is an almost exact replica of those in which Coriolanus has collided again and again with the Roman mob. For Aufidius knows as well as the Roman tribunes how to manipulate his foe for his sinister purpose. He stirs the commoners against his enemy by haranguing them on the subject of Coriolanus' perfidy:

> He has betrayed your business, and given up
> For certain drops of salt your city—Rome,
> (I say "your city") to his wife and mother;
> Breaking his oath and resolution like

> A twist of rotten silk; never admitting
> Counsel o' the war; but at his nurse's tears
> He whin'd and roar'd away your victory.   (v. v. 91–7)

In the course of this diatribe he taunts Coriolanus with epithets like "traitor" and "boy of tears," words which drive the warrior to an almost pathological seizure of rage. Then Coriolanus, shouting insults to the crowd, stirs the Volscian populace to fury. Once aroused, they rush upon him with cries of "Tear him to pieces!—Do it presently— He killed my son!—My daughter—He killed my cousin Marcus! He killed my father." The lords of Corioli, aghast at the blood-thirstiness of the mob, try in vain to calm it. But Aufidius and his conspirators have aroused the masses to the killing point. With cries of "Kill, kill, kill, kill, kill him" they fall upon Coriolanus and murder him.

This catastrophe gives final emphasis to the satiric view of Coriolanus. His automatic response to the artfully arranged provocation has at last entrapped him to his death. His end is the direct result of an over-stimulated reflex mechanism. The catastrophe of such an automaton is not tragic. It is so completely devoid of grandeur and dignity that it awakens amusement seasoned with contempt.

This derision is much less absorbing than the pity and terror provoked by a genuinely tragic denouement. For that very reason a satiric play is better suited than a tragedy to present forcefully a political exemplum. In *Coriolanus* our interest is not held by the fall of a great man destroyed by forces beyond his control. It is rather caught by the picture of social and political chaos produced both by subversive forces of democracy and by a man who is temperamentally unable to be a successful ruler. The drama, then, is a satiric representation of a slave of passion designed to teach an important political lesson.

If this is true, why has *Coriolanus* never been a popular play? The principal reason is that critics and producers have invariably regarded it as a tragedy of an orthodox but greatly inferior sort. As a tragedy it lacks, as Stoll suggests, "constructive mechanism." Neither Fate nor a villain spins the plot. Coriolanus is destroyed by what is false within his nature. Yet we do not behold the inner emotional conflict that ends in disaster. We never see the dramatic struggle taking place within his mind and spirit. Therefore his nature inevitably seems poor and shallow. More than that, all the positive qualities which he displays are offensive. The remnants of a noble pride appear darkly through a cloud of childish impatience and uncontrolled rage. Finally, his catastrophe fixes ineradicably in the minds of all who expect a tragedy an impression of Shakespeare's artistic ineptitude. Coriolanus is manipulated into a fatal crisis and he meets his end in a riot which his mad fury has precipitated. No proper tragic hero moves thus toward his end in automatic response to artfully arranged stimuli. Nor can a death which comes to a man in a wild brawl signalize any triumph of the spirit.

These are defects only if Shakespeare intended *Coriolanus* to be a tragedy of the usual sort. If he meant the play to be more satire than tragedy, most of these qualities are virtues. Shakespeare naturally avoids arousing sympathy for a man whom he wishes to deride. For this reason he fills the early scenes with trenchant speech of hostile commentators, whose business is to draw a well-rounded satiric portrait of Coriolanus. Then the author traps his victim again and again so that we may see repeatedly the writhings of his anger. Finally he artfully designs a final scene which will make his satiric intention unmistakable. The murder of Coriolanus is not the moving death of a great hero; it is the deserved result of a supreme exhibition of his folly.

The bareness of the plot of *Coriolanus* also contributes to the satiric emphasis of the drama. True to the genius of satire it keeps the minds of the spectators riveted upon the ridicule of human faults. Derision, unless associated with moral indignation, does not easily awaken aesthetic pleasure. But in *Coriolanus* ridicule has been made to serve the teaching of sound political theory and only by a few can the descriptive forces in a healthy state be strongly enough felt to moderate the discomfort which most men feel at the persistent satire of a strong man. . . .

Coriolanus: Introduction

by Harley Granville-Barker

Coriolanus cannot be ranked with the greatest of the tragedies. It lacks their transcendent vitality and metaphysical power. But while neither story nor characters evoke such qualities, those they do evoke are here in full measure. The play is notable for its craftsmanship. It is the work of a man who knows what the effect of each stroke will be, and wastes not one of them. And while ease and simplicity may sometimes be lacking, an uncertain or superfluous speech it would be hard to find. Was Shakespeare perhaps aware of some ebbing of his imaginative vitality—well there may have been after the creation in about as many years of *Othello, King Lear, Antony and Cleopatra* and *Macbeth*!—and did he purposefully choose a subject and characters which he could make the most of by judgment and skill?

The play follows close, it would seem, upon *Antony and Cleopatra.* Between the two there is the general likeness of a setting in Roman history. For the rest, the contrasts are so many and so marked as hardly to be fortuitous. To that large picture of an imperial Rome and a decadent Egypt and of

> The triple pillar of the world transformed
> Into a strumpet's fool

succeeds this story of earlier and austerer days, of a Rome still challengeable by her neighbours and of a very different hero. Antony and Caius Marcius are men of action both. But Antony is the astute politician too, and by that talent could save himself from disaster if he would—does save himself and has the game in his hands, only to throw it way because

> The beds i' the East are soft.

"Coriolanus: *Introduction.*" From **Prefaces to Shakespeare** *by Harley Granville-Barker (Princeton: Princeton University Press, 1946; London: Sidgwick and Jackson Ltd., 1947), vol. 3, 93–99. Copyright 1946 by Princeton University Press. Reprinted by permission of Princeton University Press and Field Fisher & Co.*

Antony—and Othello and Macbeth too—are soldiers, famous generals;
but that is not the side of them we come to know. Coriolanus is the
man of action seen in action, and among the heroes of the maturer
canon unique in this.[1] He is the younger man, a fighter, and a brilliant
one, but effectively no more. He is at heart—and despite his trials remains to the end—the incorrigible boy, with "Boy" for the final insult
flung at him by Aufidius that he will at no price swallow. And save in
physical valour (of which in the elder, by the plan of the action, we
hear but see nothing), in every trait he and Antony radically differ. To
the one his men are "my good fellows." He jokes with them, praises
them impulsively and generously for their pluck. The other is curt,
even to friends and equals, self-conscious, and incapable of the least
appeal to the populace he despises. In his contempt for spoils and rewards, in his stubbornness, his aristocratic pride, in his chastity—Virgilia greeting him on his minatory return, it is

> Now by the jealous queen of heaven, that kiss
> I carried from thee, dear; and my true lip
> Hath virgined it ever since

—in every significant feature the two stand contrasted.

Then in Cleopatra's place we have Volumnia; for the exotic mistress
the Roman mother. Yet each in her fashion brings ruin, to lover or
son. And for the Egyptian Court, in which, says Enobarbus

> Mine, and most of our fortunes tonight
> Shall be—drunk to bed,

we exchange that picture of the simple Roman home, its great ladies
content to

> *sit themselves down on two low stools*
> *and sew.*

The contrasts are pervasive too. In the one play the action is spa-
cious and varied beyond comparison; Shakespeare's every resource is
drawn upon, his invention finds full scope. In *Coriolanus* it is disciplined, kept to its single channel, and the story moves lucidly and directly to its retributive end. And in one major difference most of the
rest are rooted: in the part played in each by the idea of Rome. In
each, of course, it is a vital part. Antony early forecasts his own ruin
in that reckless

> Let Rome in Tiber melt, and the wide arch
> Of the ranged empire fall.

---

[1] And even Henry V, at war, is not seen fighting. He is the didactic hero, and
this is far less mature dramatic work.

Cleopatra's first note of alarm lest she lose him sounds in the

> He was disposed to mirth; but on the sudden
> A Roman thought has struck him

and throughout she is a prey to her jealousy, hatred and dread of
Rome. Still, this is little more than a background for the personal passion. But in *Coriolanus* everything centres upon Rome. It is the play's
one sounding-board. The springs of the action are there. Coriolanus
himself sinks at last by comparison to something like second place. He
returns for his revenge, and all thoughts and eyes are on him. He departs, self-defeated; and it is Volumnia who re-enters the city in triumph, hailed by a

> Behold our patroness, the life of Rome!

And his death thereafter in Corioles even approaches anti-climax.

But this fidelity to the larger, less personal theme lends the play a
very Roman strength and solidity, which compensates to some degree,
and in its kind, for the lack of such plenary inspiration as has given
us Lear or Macbeth, colossal and stripped to the soul. The play gains
strength too from the keying of its action throughout to strife of one
sort or another. Of no other of the plays can it be said that, but for
an incidental scene or so, and for the stilled suspense in which we listen to Volumnia's ultimate pleadings, the quarrelling and fighting
scarcely cease from beginning to end. It is dramatically the more important, then, that the opposing stresses should be kept fairly balanced,
in sympathy as well as in force. Amid mere ebb and flow of violence
the interest of the action could not be sustained. But the balance is
adjusted and continually readjusted, the tension never quite relaxed.
And the skill of the play's workmanship shows largely in this.

The story allows for scene after scene of actual fighting, and Shakespeare contrives for these every sort of variety: ranging in the war with
the Volscians from the amazing sight of Marcius pitted against a whole
city-full to the duel with Aufidius; in the struggle with the citizens
from the victory where, sword in hand, he leads a handful of his
friends against the rabble—a victory he is persuaded not to pursue—
to the defeat in which this same rabble, better disciplined by the Tribunes, combine to banish him. And in the play's closing passages the
happy shouts of the Romans, freed from their fears, are contrasted
with the spurious triumph of the Volscians.

The balance of sympathy also is fairly adjusted, neither side captur-
ing—and keeping—overmuch. Shakespeare has been freely charged, in
an age apt to be prejudiced in its favour, with bias against the populace. Allow for a little harmless ridicule and it is really not so. They
are no match for Menenius in a contest of wit—although one of them,

to his surprise, gamely stands up to him—but they see through Marcius' mockery, for all that they are too polite to tell him so. In that scene of the "garment of humility," indeed, his manners contrast most unfavorably with theirs. Individually, they seem simple, kindly creatures; collectively, they are doubtless unwise and unstable. They are human. Marcius has been their enemy, and they do not forget it. He declares that he remains so, and when he attacks them, they retaliate. They follow their leaders blindly, are misled and turn on them savagely at last. It is not a very sentimental survey, certainly. But why should it be?

The Tribunes are left the unqualified "villains of the piece"; a surface of comic colouring—which by making them amusingly contemptible may make them a little less detestable—is the only mitigation allowed them. But not one of the characters with a capital share in the mellay of the action is very sympathetically drawn. Not, certainly,

> worthy Menenius Agrippa; one that
> hath always loved the people

—so acclaimed by them at our first sight of him, but in fact, as we soon find, cajoling them and sneering at them by turns. Not Aufidius, unstable in good and ill. The untender Volumnia remains so to the last, heedless in her triumph of the price her son must pay for it; a point made implicitly only, but clearly enough to leave us feeling cold towards her. And Shakespeare treats Caius Marcius himself detachedly, as a judge might, without creative warmth. Both sides of his case are to be heard; and we see him first at his worst (an unusual introduction for a titular hero) bullying the hungry citizens. The balance is soon adjusted by evidence—the fighter seen actually fighting—that his valour exceeds all tales of it; in battle and after it he stands out as hero supreme. And his trial of character, when this begins, is lifted, at its crisis, to high ground. It is not his ill-conditioned egoism but his fervent championship of an unpopular faith that gets him driven from Rome. The balance shifts violently when he seeks recreant revenge for this, to be shifted again when at the last moment he abandons it and pays the penalty. Finally, something like justice is done.

The play's range of characters is not a wide one, for it is kept closely relevant to the demands of the action, and these do not by much overspread the direct channel of the story. But within this range Shakespeare works with complete surety. We have that most leisurely of openings, the tale of the Belly and the Members, and Marcius' first attack on the citizens—much of a distractingly different sort having to happen before that full quarrel is joined—is given good scope. The geography of the battle scenes by Corioles is schemed for us as concisely as clearly. But we have their action at length; for this serves to fill out the characters of Marcius, of Cominius and Titus Lartius too, each the more himself by contrast with the others; the prudent Consul, the old warrior so young at heart, who will

> lean upon one crutch and fight with t'other
> Ere stay behind this business

generously happy, both of them, in their arrogant young hero's glory. The dispute that leads to the banishment is thrashed out at fullest length, argued back and forth, and yet again, nothing significant left uncanvassed. Later, in the scene at Antium, which brings us the renegade Coriolanus, we note that Shakespeare gives as much space to the sly, flunkey commentings of Aufidius' servants upon the amazing business and their master's romantic aberration as he has to the encounter itself. This, besides lowering the tension, helps resolve the new combination into the unheroic key in which it will be worked out.

Shakespeare has now come to ask for more sheer acting from his actors than he did, for more meaning and feeling to be compressed occasionally into half a dozen words than would once have flowed from a rhetorical hundred, for expressive listening as well as expressive speech, for silence itself sometimes to be made eloquent.

Holds her by the hand silent

—the play's most tragic moment, in which Marcius accepts defeat and in the sequel death at his mother's hand, confided to a simple stage direction.[2] Throughout the play action and words are expressively keyed together, the action of as great an import as the words. Marcius' share in the scene of the wearing of the gown of humility is as much picturing as speaking; and the mere sight of him later in his Roman dress, surrounded by the Volsces in theirs, sitting in council with them, marching into Corioles at their head—the graphic discord vivifies the play's ending.[3] The sight of the silently approaching figures of Volumnia, Virgilia and Valeria makes double effect; directly upon us, and upon us again through the effect made upon

---

[2] And it is pretty certainly Shakespeare's own. Such moments of eloquent silence are to be found indicated, more or less explicitly, in all the later plays. A very notable one comes with Macbeth's hearing of his wife's death. Another follows upon the blow that Othello publicly deals Desdemona.

[3] In *Cymbeline*, certainly, costume marks the difference between Roman and British, and in *Macbeth* between Scots and English; in *Antony and Cleopatra*, probably, between Roman and Egyptian. We may take for granted, I think, that Volscians and Romans were dressed distinctively. A "realistic" reading may suggest that Marcius would cast off his Roman garb with his allegiance. But I believe that, quitting the "mean apparel" in which he went to encounter Aufidius, he would re-appear as a Roman general, the dramatic effect being worth more than any logic.

Marcius. And little though Virgilia says (and Valeria not a word),
Volumnia so insistently joins them to her plea that their simple
presence has an all-but-articulate value; while the actual spectacle of
Marcius fighting single-handed "within Corioles gates" is better witness to his prowess than any of the "acclamations hyperbolical" which
he somewhat self-consciously decries. The memory of it, moreover, will
not fade, only lie dormant until at the last it is re-kindled by the
magnificently trenchant

> "Boy!" false hound!
> If you have writ your annals true, 'tis there,
> That, like an eagle in a dove-cote, I
> Fluttered your Volscians in Corioli;
> Alone I did it.

Here, then, we have a play of action dealing with men of action;
and in none that Shakespeare wrote do action and character better
supplement and balance each other.

Roads to Freedom: *Coriolanus*

by Donald A. Stauffer

. . . As in *Antony and Cleopatra,* the purpose of this play is made
certain by the structure. Such ambiguities as it possesses are con-
sciously developed; they are not careless inconsistencies, but parts of
the ironic comprehensiveness of the author's vision. The welfare of
the state is the basic standard, to which every action is ultimately referred. Coriolanus, its chief defender, is flawed in character; his defects and qualities are explicitly assessed in accordance with a conventional theory of tragedy. The whole production is given coherence
and clarity by the dominating metaphor of the body and its parts, by
imagery selected from the work-a-day world and sauced with Roman
details from Plutarch, and by a formal concentration, proportioning,
and ordering of the scenes.[1] Shakespeare may well have admired the
antiquarian accuracy and dramatic economy of his friend Ben Jonson
in *Sejanus,* and may have determined to add such virtues to his own
scene-making.

Rome—"the Roman state," "the country," "our country," "thy
country"—is the hero of this play. In one sense Rome is not so
much a *patria* as a *matria,* like the England of the history plays:

"Roads to Freedom: Coriolanus." *From* Shakespeare's World of Images *by Donald
A. Stauffer (New York: W. W. Norton & Company, Inc., 1949), pp. 252–65. Copyright 1949 by W. W. Norton & Company, Inc. Reprinted by permission of the
publisher. This selection has been abridged for this volume.*

[1] See, for instance, the certain ordering of the initial scenes: in the first, Coriolanus is presented as "chief enemy to the people" (who are already mutinous), and
as a great soldier; in the second the theme of external dangers to the state is introduced; while the third inserts the familial theme before the act is allowed to
proceed in multiple scenes designed to demonstrate Coriolanus' greatness as a
soldier. See also the middle act, in which the middle scene centers on Volumnia's
power to persuade her son (an exquisite preparation for the crucial climactic scene
of V, iii), and is cradled between the two parallel scenes of Coriolanus' flaring up
against the people. Act V builds toward its climax by having the unsuccessful
embassies of Cominius and of Menenius precede Volumnia's successful attempt;
and the procession of Virgilia, Volumnia, Valeria, young Marcius, with attendants,
is given a formal choric accompaniment in an odd sort of pageant-soliloquy delivered by Coriolanus (V, iii, 22–33).

> This nurse, this teeming womb of royal kings, . . .
> Dear for her reputation through the world.

Volumnia is one projection of "the country, our dear nurse"—so that when she gloweringly imagines that Coriolanus may "triumphantly tread on thy country's ruin" and in succeeding lines that he may "tread on thy mother's womb that brought thee to this world," the two ideas are interchangeable. But in another metaphor, the dominant image of the play is of the great impersonal body of Menenius' opening parable. Shakespeare expands what he finds in North's Plutarch until the body politic of the fable controls the thought of the play; and the harmony of all its parts, interdependent and interacting, becomes the virtuous end of all deeds.[2]

Menenius in his fable upholds the politic view of common sense. Like so many of Shakespeare's old counsellors, he is too ripe in wisdom and compromise; he sees so much that he loses the name of action. Between the rabble-rousing tribunes and the bluntly contemptuous Coriolanus, the old senator is impotent.

Coriolanus is presented as the soul of the Roman republic. His political theory, if it could be separated from his personality, is admirably noble and altruistic. In his own mind, he is the servant of a state in which all citizens should be servants. Yet his idealism is uncompromising. He gives again the old answer to the old question: What would happen if someone told the truth? In politics—at least in Rome and in Shakespeare—absolute truth-telling will not work.

Coriolanus is modest because he is the servant of the state. In Shakespeare's iridescent thought, such a statement is not the whole truth; and often enough this modesty is presented as a trick of inverted pride, so that Coriolanus sounds as conventional as a football captain before a microphone.[3] Yet there is principle back of his

[2] For the fable of the body, see I, i, 92–167. None of the body's parts—not "the kingly-crowned head, the vigilant eye, the counsellor heart, the arm our soldier, our steed the leg, the tongue our trumpeter, with other muniments and petty helps in this our fabric"—is self-sufficient. They may feel that they are the instruments that "see and hear, devise, instruct, walk, feel, and mutually participate"; they may believe that taken together they "minister unto the appetite and affection common to the whole body." But the mutinous members must not revolt against the belly, the source of sustenance to be sent through the blood. The belly of the state is the senate, grave and good and deliberate, "the storehouse and the shop of the whole body," which passes on to its "incorporate friends" "that natural competency whereby they live." The health of this great body of the Roman state must not be endangered, whether by insurrection of members against the belly, or by the belly itself, or by the "great toe" of its plebeian leader, or by its own ascetically sublimated spirit in Coriolanus.

[3] As one example, see his automatic answer to the senators' extolling of his wounds before the populace: "Scratches with briers, Scars to move laughter only" (III, iii, 51–52).

brushing aside the recounting of his exploits—"Will the time serve to
tell? I do not think." He sees himself and others as natural parts of
a common effort: "I have done As you have done—that's what I can."
And he renounces a special share of booty in order to stand upon his
"common part." He had rather have his head scratched in the sun
than hear his nothings monstered, and precipitately he leaves the
stage when he is about to be praised. Cominius, knowing that a state
should reward merit in its citizens, may be right in reproving his
young lieutenant for too much modesty and for too much cruelty to
his good name: "You shall not be The grave of your deserving." But
the cunning tribunes are surely wrong in their analysis of Caius
Marcius' acceptance of a subordinate position under Cominius; their
motive-hunting reveals only their own foxships. Caius Marcius acted
as a soldier, whose satisfaction and pride spring from a job well
done. He "rewards His deeds with doing them."

Coriolanus is the watchdog of Rome. Or in terms of the images
in the play, he is not the "lamb that baes like a bear" as the tribunes
would have him, but the "bear indeed, that lives like a lamb" as
Menenius sees him. He clamors and fights only against those who, as
he sees it, would destroy the state. Service is all he desires—not
power.[4] But the service must be on his terms. Though he shudders
away from appearing before the undeserving populace, his response
to the senate upon being made consul is unaffected and simple:

> I do owe them still
> My life and services.   (II, ii, 137–38)

Before the respected senators, therefore, he will passionately plead
that they must not throw away the safety and health of Rome because
of fear or lenity or ignorance. The whole of the third act is a
tumultuous presentation of clashing theories of governance. When
Coriolanus is unprovoked, his prayer for Rome glows with noble
sincerity:

> Th' honour'd gods
> Keep Rome in safety, and the chairs of justice
> Supplied with worthy men! plant love among 's!
> Throng our large temples with the shows of peace
> And not our streets with war!   (III, iii, 33–37)

But he is constantly provoked—by the tribunes who place the good

---

[4] The idea of service is underlined in the following passages: "To gratify his
noble serivce" (Menenius, II, ii, 44); "They ne'er did service . . . This kind of service . . ." (Coriolanus, III, i, 122, 124); "What do *you* prate of service?" (Coriolanus
to Brutus, III, iii, 83); "I'll do his country service" (Coriolanus, IV, iv, 26); "my
revengeful services . . . to do thee service" (Coriolanus, IV, v, 94, 106).

of their class and their own personal power above the welfare of
Rome. Coriolanus fails to see how they play upon his own personal
weaknesses. The senators in turn fail to see the fundamental political
weakness that is opening a chasm in the state. Coriolanus talks to the
air. The senators are good but most unwise, grave but reckless; their
softness is dangerous. As the tribunes, those Tritons of the minnows,
move toward absolute power, Coriolanus poses an unanswerable dilemma: "You are plebeians If they be senators."

> When two authorities are up,
> Neither supreme, how soon confusion
> May enter 'twixt the gap of both and take
> The one by th' other.   (III, i, 109–12)

Coriolanus' conception of the state is not left for speculation. It is
developed fully, with all its reasons and purposes. To grant privileges
to the citizens, instead of exacting services, is to nourish disobedience
and feed the ruin of the state. *Panem et circenses!* Such temporizing
gifts to the clamorous multitude debase the nature of government,
and will only be interpreted as the concessions of fear. "We are the
greater poll." The well-proportioned figure of the state will turn into
a megacephalic idiot. This "double worship" of conflicting governing powers can only increase the opposition between disdainful
patricians and insulting plebeians. The genuine needs of government
will come to depend upon unstable slightness, when action can be
concluded only "by the yea and no of general ignorance." "Nothing
is done to purpose." Those "that love the fundamental part of state"
must therefore take radical action to rescind the mistakes precipitated
by emergency and rebellion. They must restore a responsible and
unified authority, and "Let what is meet be said it must be meet."

This patrician's idealism, which escapes being despotism only because it is based on the firm conviction that the senators are the born
and trained servants of the state, is too extreme for practical politics.
Temperance, when it is presented in the play, goes unheeded in the
conflict for absolute authority. Coriolanus "cannot temp'rately trans-
port his honours." "Being once chaf'd, he cannot Be rein'd again to
temperance." "Nay, temperately! Your promise," says Menenius just
before Coriolanus' wildest outburst. And the old senator ruefully remembers that Rome, peaceful for a moment under the exultant
tribunes, might have been much better if Coriolanus "could have
temporiz'd." It is impossible. Coriolanus' intolerant altruism clashes
against the opposite extremes of popular appetite; the city is unbuilt
and laid flat; violent ideals generate opposed violent action; and as
the rabble shouts "Down with him! down with him!" against Corio-

lanus, poor Menenius disappears in the maelstrom with the disregarded advice of "On both sides more respect."

Nevertheless, Shakespeare's conservative and aristocratic cast of mind takes its own pleasure in shaping events. He goes out of his way to develop an incident to show that Coriolanus does not hate the people and the poor as a class, but the sloth, vacillation, stupidity, and greed which he finds so frequently among them: the only gift that Coriolanus begs of his general after the victory at Corioles is freedom for "a poor man," "my poor host," a stranger among the Antiates whose very name Coriolanus in his weariness cannot recall. The voice of the people is doubled in triviality, halved in dignity, by being assigned to the indistinguishable twin tribunes Brutus and Sicinius. The plebeians themselves are dangerous—not less so because they are often well-meaning. They are again and again allowed to speak like kindergarten pupils or morons:

> Ingratitude is monstrous; and for the multitude to be ingrateful were
> to make a monster of the multitude, of the which we being members,
> should bring ourselves to be monstrous members.   (II, iii, 10–14)

The unsteady people and the villainous tribunes are sketched in to the verge of caricature. The final touch is given in workmanlike fashion when a civil servant, an impartial spectator, is allowed to say that Coriolanus' "noble carelessness" frankly reveals to the people "the *true knowledge* he has in their disposition."

Yet Shakespeare's even-handed justice, his sense of the almost infinite complexity of any specific moral decision—or his superb dramatic sensitivity, which is much the same thing—compels him to put in caveats and demurrers. In these later plays, Shakespeare is steadily moving toward a world where the important values lie entirely within the individual mind. The inner and outer worlds are therefore sharply separated. This is true even in this subtlest of his political studies of the state. It is true even while Coriolanus stands for consul in the Forum, and the electors dissolve into air, into thin air: thirty times in a single scene they become no more than "voices," voices, voices. It is true even while we see the great body of Rome turn into a thousand-tongued monster tettered with measles, a many-headed multitude, a Hydra. It is true at the turning-point of the play, when the absolute popular "shall" overwhelms reason and banishes Rome's defender as "enemy to the people and his country." Coriolanus turns on all Rome and says in his magnificence: "You common cry of curs, . . . I banish you!" In order to make his portrait of Coriolanus a pure demonstration of inner conflicts Shakespeare stacks the evidence: the popular cause is shown as stupid, sordid, and selfish; Corio-

lanus is given a nobly unassailable theory of government. He banishes
Rome and withdraws into "a world elsewhere." Within his own nature
he finds defeat and victory.

Once the problem is so set, Shakespeare does not spare his hero.
Though Coriolanus may be granted "true knowledge" of the people's
fickleness by one spectator, another immediately answers: "To seem
to affect the malice and displeasure of the people is as bad as that
which he dislikes—to flatter them for their love." Cominius has already reproved him at length for his impatient modesty. His impassioned plea for the safety of the state is broken across by the
comment:

> You speak o' th' people
> As if you were a god to punish, not
> A man of their infirmity.   (III, i, 80–82)

Does the hero act in choler or within reason? Even in the words of
praise at the end, as his "noble corse" is borne off to the sound of a
dead march, we are reminded of "his own impatience."

His integrity seems absolute. "He is himself alone." Coriolanus
will not divide himself with the world. Though the world may be
filled with beggars and cowards and curs, it is dangerous to call them
by their names. Nor is it charitable. Coriolanus remains adamant; he
is "what he cannot help in his nature"; he will be the people's servant
in his own way or no servant at all. He cannot be ruled; he cannot
dissemble with his nature as his mother can with hers; he cannot
understand why his friends would have him false to his beliefs; his
attempt to exchange his disposition for a "harlot's spirit" must
obviously end in failure because of the very mood in which it is
undertaken; he thinks continually of the "sign of what you are." His
narrow rigidity is summarized clearly in Aufidius' formal character
sketch, which points out his

> nature
> Not to be other than one thing, not moving
> From th' casque to th' cushion, but commanding peace
> Even with the same austerity and garb
> As he controll'd the war.   (IV, vii, 41–45)

He mars his fortune because "His nature is too noble for the
world." His greatest lovers—Menenius, Volumnia, Aufidius—in the
very heart of their admiration are aware that pure nobility may itself
be a disastrous extreme. Volumnia tells him flatly:

> You are too absolute;
> Though therein you can never be too noble
> But when extremities speak.   (III, ii, 39–41)

His mother, out of ambition for her son, gives him worldly advice, though it dishonors her more to beg of him than for him to beg of the people:

> You might have been enough the man you are
> With striving less to be so.   (III, ii, 19–20)

Yet they cannot help glorying in his excess. Volumnia flaunts the tribunes:

> As far as doth the Capitol exceed
> The meanest house in Rome, so far my son . . .
> Whom you have banish'd does exceed you all.

To Aufidius, embracing him as dearer than a wedded mistress, he is "most absolute sir." And Aufidius, even when he has become jealous of Coriolanus' prowess as an ally, must admit:

> I think he'll be to Rome
> As is the osprey to the fish, who takes it
> By sovereignty of nature.   (IV, vii, 33–35)

Whatever may be his particular fault, Aufidius knows that "he has a merit To choke it in the utt'rance."

His merits admitted, Shakespeare seeks from beginning to end for the tragic fault. At the very start, one of the citizens sees that the people need not thank Coriolanus for his service, since "he pays himself with being proud." And as for his military accomplishment, "he did it to please his mother and to be partly proud, which he is, even to the altitude of his virtue." In formal summation, before the final trial of his nature, Aufidius scrutinizes the character of his great foe. It is characteristic of Shakespeare that the tragic flaw is not to be reduced to a single ruling passion, but is multiplied into several hypotheses:

> Whether 'twas pride,
> Which out of daily fortune ever taints
> The happy man; whether defect of judgment,
> To fail in the disposing of those chances
> Which he was lord of; or whether nature,
> Not to be other than one thing, . . . but one of these
> (As he hath spices of them all, not all,
> For I dare so far free him) made him fear'd,
> So hated, and so banish'd.   (IV, vii. 37–48

Pride? Lack of policy? Intransigence? Or some hypothetical combination among them?

It is also characteristic of Shakespeare that the last catastrophe

results from a far more tragic theme than the textbook punishing
of peccadilloes. Shakespeare reverts to his conception—it was clearly
present in *King John,* and embryonic even in *The Two Gentlemen of
Verona*—that the truly tragic choice is between two irreconcilable
goods, one of which must be abandoned. He prepares for Coriolanus'
decision by displaying Volumnia's parallel decision. She compels him
to think with himself "How more unfortunate than all living women"
is her feminine embassy in their divided allegiances. Her painful
choice is presented in such certain balance and with such driving
reiteration that it must be quoted in full:

> For how can *we,*
> Alas, how *can* we for our country pray,
> *Whereto we are bound,* together with thy victory,
> *Whereto we are bound?* Alack, *or* we must lose
> The country, our dear nurse, *or else* thy person,
> Our comfort in the country. We must find
> An evident calamity, though we *had*
> Our wish, which side should win; for *either* thou
> Must as a foreign recreant be led
> With manacles through our streets, *or else*
> Triumphantly tread on thy country's ruin
> And bear the palm for having bravely shed
> Thy wife and children's blood.   (V, iii, 106–18)

How can Shakespeare make credible a tragic split in a character
of such unyielding integrity as that of Coriolanus? To answer such
a question one must turn back through the play to see the little tricks
by which a full personality is revealed. Coriolanus has made himself
into the professional soldier. He hurriedly throws off the gown of
humility in order that he may know himself again, for his armed knees
bow but in his stirrup. He does not care for the good opinion of
amateurs, but for Aufidius, the second soldier of the world—"Spoke
he of me?" The emulation between these two is played up throughout: Coriolanus wishes for another war that he might again drive
Aufidius from the field; and Aufidius views his rival with varying
admiration and jealousy. When Coriolanus defeats him—the fore-
warning comes in the first act—Aufidius will give up his honor for
wrath or craft, in order that he may wash his "fierce hands in 's
heart."

Yet Coriolanus is so absolute in his soldiership that he cannot be
defeated in arms. He is the "flower of warriors." He knows that "brave
death outweighs bad life," and that his country is dearer than himself. Death lies in his "nervy arm"; his sword is "death's stamp"; he
is "a thing of blood" and strikes Corioles "like a planet." The first

third of the play is given over to the exaltation of Rome's defender, until it seems undeniable that "valour is the chiefest virtue and Most dignifies the haver." He drives himself and others unsparingly. The soldiers before Corioles know how impossible an example he may set for others to follow, and he is rough on those closest to him even in jocular triumph: he greets his wife as "My gracious silence," and turns to his antiquated friend Menenius with the words: "And live you yet?"

Even his language is in the lineage of the Shakespearean soldiers— Philip the Bastard, Hotspur, King Harry, Enobarbus—and modifies by attraction the diction of the entire play. To the flourish of trumpets and the sound of drums he is ceremoniously hailed by his new-won name of Caius Marcius Coriolanus. He answers:

> I will go wash.

When his old friend counsels him to speak courteously to the citizens, his impulse is to "Bid them wash their faces And keep their teeth clean." Contrasted with the glow of war, the ground-images of the play are drawn from the hearth, the family, and small homely events.

The thoroughbred has had training as well as breeding. The tribunes themselves are aware not only of the long line of his noble ancestors, but also "How youngly he began to serve his country." Cominius recounts his exploits at the age of sixteen, when he entered "his pupil age" as a man. His mother has devoted her life to fostering his warlike traits. The comeliness of youth was not enough for the only son of her womb: she was pleased to let him seek danger. With a more than Spartan savagery, she exults in the renown, honor, and fame of her "man-child." "To a cruel war I sent him." From his mother he had learned that brave death outweighs bad life—for she professes sincerely: "had I a dozen sons, each in my love alike, and none less dear than thine and my good Marcius, I had rather had eleven die nobly for their country than one voluptuously surfeit out of action." Her contempt for all cowards, Romans or Volscians, that run from her son's exploits "as children from a bear," her magnifying of her son's sole valor, rise to a vertiginous dream of slaughter and a grim picture of her son as death the reaper:

> His bloody brow
> With his mail'd hand then wiping, forth he goes,
> Like to a harvestman that's task'd to mow
> Or all or lose his hire.   (I, iii, 37–40)

And when Coriolanus' wife shudders at the imagination of blood, his mother scornfully turns her aside:

> Away, you fool! It more becomes a man
> Than gilt his trophy. The breasts of Hecuba
> When she did suckle Hector, look'd not lovelier
> Than Hector's forehead when it spit forth blood
> At Grecian sword, contemning.

Blood and mother's milk are mingled, and we are prepared for Valeria's miniature of the young Marcius, "the father's son," who in his rage at falling down in the pursuit of a butterfly, sets his teeth and tears the butterfly to pieces. His grandmother remarks complacently: "One on 's father's moods."

This young boy Marcius (perhaps the youngest character with a speaking part in all of Shakespeare's plays) is no accidental addition. He is the needed symbol of a developing theme. He is "a poor epitome of yours" as Volumnia reminds Coriolanus, urging the boy to speak because

> Perhaps thy childishness will move him more
> Than can our reasons.   (V, iii, 157–58)

And as the whole family plead before the avenging soldier, the boy's one speech contains all of his father's fighting independent spirit:

> 'A shall not tread on me!
> I'll run away till I am bigger, but then I'll fight.

There is something boyish about Coriolanus' honor and bravery and anger and stubborn temper.[5]

If Coriolanus is to be swayed from the vengeful purpose which he has deliberately fostered in himself, it must be because of something deeper, more elemental and primal and atavistic, than rational argument. It need not be something great—for the asp in *Antony and Cleopatra*, the handkerchief in *Othello*, has shown "What poor an instrument may do a noble deed!" (or an ignoble). Coriolanus himself knows the "slippery turns" of the world, which may alter the destinies of states "by some chance, Some trick not worth an egg." In the deciding moment, his resolve turns upon his boyish relations with his mother. He had been bewildered and hurt that his mother had not approved his actions before the plebeians; he shrank from her chiding, and for her sake and her praises, he tried to change his

---

[5] Even the plebeians carry on the theme with their childish arguments, and are reproved by Coriolanus himself, in dramatic irony, for giving him only "children's voices" (III, i, 30). A richer texture is added by hidden references, as when Coriolanus in disguise thinks of himself slain "in puny battle" by "wives with spits and boys with stones" (IV, iv, 5–6), and Cominius catches up the anecdote of the young Marcius with: "they follow him against us brats with no less confidence than boys pursuing summer butterflies or butchers killing flies" (IV, vi, 92–95).

nature: in a tantrum of rage he resolved to act "mildly." Now, with supreme dramatic irony, he is shown instinctively expecting his mother at the very moment he has determined to see no further embassies from the city. He can resist all her arguments that glance at his honor and integrity, for he has fought them out within himself. He steadies himself by swearing that determination shall subdue warm impulse:

> I'll never
> Be such a gosling to obey instinct, but stand
> As if a man were author of himself
> And knew no other kin.   (V, iii, 34–37)

But he is not self-sufficient; he is still bound to his mother; he has no answer but silence when she turns scold and dares to assume the last posture, so unnatural for her, of pitying herself. The trick not worth an egg is played in the image of a mother hen clucking at her chicks:

> Thou hast never in thy life
> Show'd thy dear mother any courtesy,
> When she (poor hen), fond of no second brood,
> Has cluck'd thee to the wars, and safely home
> Loaden with honour.

He learns pity from the mother who has taught him to be pitiless. His choice is made clear-eyed: Rome will live even though its sons and daughters are trodden upon. So also that miniature of the state, the human family, is greater than any of its members:

> O my mother, mother! O!
> You have won a happy victory to Rome;
> But for your son—believe it, O believe it!—
> Most dangerously you have with him prevail'd,
> If not most mortal to him. But let it come.

The tragic choice between two goods is formally underlined by the witnessing Aufidius in an aside:

> I am glad thou hast set thy mercy and thy honour
> At difference in thee. Out of that I'll work
> Myself a former fortune.

The temporal victory of the smaller man over the greater is brought about by a touching again upon the quick of the hero's nature, and by weighing the little things not worth an egg against the affairs of the world. Three times Aufidius displays to the Volscians the balanced scales:

> At a few drops of women's rheum, which are
> As cheap as lies, he sold the blood and labour
> Of our great action. Therefore shall he die.
>
> He has betray'd your business and given up,
> For certain drops of salt, your city Rome
> (I say "your city") to his wife and mother.
>
>   at his nurse's tears
> He whin'd and roar'd away your victory.

Though in the tragic inner world a tear may be worth all that is won or lost, it cannot answer in Corioles. Coriolanus defends himself by calling upon the war-god, but Aufidius' answering taunt compresses into a single line the moral complexities of the whole action:

> Name not the god, thou boy of tears!

"Boy! . . . Boy! . . . Boy!" Coriolanus cries, and loses himself in the same rage of hurt pride which his son displayed in mammocking the butterfly to pieces. The childish fury is all that Aufidius needs, and to cries of "Tear him to pieces!" "He kill'd my son!" "He kill'd my father!" the conspirators dispatch Marcius, and Aufidius stands on the body. For the last time, Shakespeare has set inner integrity in tragic contrast to the slippery turns of the world. For the last time the dying hero has returned to his earliest instincts and deepest loyalties. For the last time Shakespeare has used his image of a nature too noble for the world destroyed by its very magnanimity, its death closed over by the life of the worldlings. The long procession is finished—Henry IV after Richard, Antony after Caesar, and Octavius after Antony, Fortinbras succeeding Hamlet, and Cassio Othello, and Albany Lear.

Yet the vistas of freedom may be seen even by the earthbound. The ideal of a perfect state may be held and defended in a city of apron-men and garlic-eaters. Integrity of purpose may still be translated into action and be admired. At the painful moment of choice, it may even rise above itself in a realization of blood brotherhood, in the acceptance of the human family for its miserable weaknesses and thwarted desires as well as for its capacities and aspirations. Human solidarity is such a final good that Shakespeare is even willing to extol war above peace in transient speculations, for peace "makes men hate one another. Reason: because they then less need one another." No man is author of himself, nor can any man afford to know no kin. The strongest man must learn to kneel. And if in these plays there are no gods beyond himself to kneel before, then he must kneel to himself in others. Shakespeare's tragic world stretches as far as the human eye can see in height and width, its vertical warp of passion held firmly in place by the horizontal weaving of compassion.

Shakespeare's Tragic Frontier: *Coriolanus*

by Willard Farnham

In *Coriolanus,* Shakespeare finds within deeply flawed yet noble human character the only tragic mystery that really matters, just as he does in *Antony and Cleopatra.* He also focuses attention narrowly upon a single example, as he does not in *Antony and Cleopatra.* The tragic flaw of the hero reveals itself at the very beginning of the action, and once we have seen it we never wonder whether we have seen it aright. It is constantly in evidence, first as Coriolanus rises to an eminence from which he can reach for the Roman consulship, then as he mars his fortune and enters upon a downward course, and finally as he goes to his destruction.

The hero does not merely stand at the center of the tragedy; he *is* the tragedy. He brings no one down with him in his fall, and his character is entirely sufficient to explain his fall. No supernatural forces are shown to be at work against him. The tribunes and Aufidius work underhandedly to entrap and undo him, but it seems that by taking advantage of the imperfections of his nature they only hurry him into making tragic errors which eventually he would have made of his own accord. The tragic flaw of Coriolanus is pride, as we are told by other characters in the play again and again. The paradox of Coriolanus is that in his pride, or closely connected with it, there is not only everything bad but also everything good by which he comes to be a subject for Shakespearean tragedy.

Shakespeare took from the moral Plutarch the conception of Coriolanus as a notable combination of good and bad qualities, but he changed radically the nature of the combination. He intensified the drama involved in the opposition between the two sets of qualities by binding them much more closely together than Plutarch had bound them. It was Shakespeare himself who created the paradox in Coriolanus, and he did so by making the good and the bad in his

"*Shakespeare's Tragic Frontier:* Coriolanus." *From* Shakespeare's Tragic Frontier: The World of His Final Tragedies *by Willard Farnham (Berkeley: University of California Press, 1950), pp. 207–8, 211–19, 263–64. Copyright 1950 by the Regents of the University of California. Reprinted by permission of the publisher. The chapter has been abridged for this volume.*

character into elements seemingly inseparable and even seemingly interdependent. . . .

Thus, as Plutarch sees it, there was nothing paradoxical about the nobility of spirit shown by Coriolanus. His good qualities were thoroughly good and his bad thoroughly bad, and the two sets of qualities were quite separate. His honesty, temperance, and valor had sufficient power in themselves and drew no strength from his insolent haughtiness, which was purely a failing. Plutarch very obviously thinks that these virtues could have existed in Coriolanus, and could have shown to better advantage, if the haughtiness had been absent, for the haughtiness was merely unpolished roughness and had a train of anger that was merely impatience. It was not this haughtiness but his "great harte" that stirred up the courage of Coriolanus and made him do notable deeds. The separation between his good and bad qualities was all the more distinct because they had separate origins: the good existed because of his heredity and the bad because of the environment of his youth. Certainly Plutarch wants his readers to see the faults of Coriolanus plainly and to draw a moral lesson from them, but he gives the impression that the good characteristics of Coriolanus are the natural man—the true man—and that the bad ones are accidentally acquired. The faults of Shakespeare's Coriolanus are much more deeply rooted than those of Plutarch's Coriolanus.

It was entirely possible for a man of the European Renaissance to be blind to the faults of Coriolanus and to see in his story an example of the envy and hatred that human mediocrity all too frequently feels toward those who are set apart in the world by greatness of spirit; for to one type of Renaissance mind it might seem that Coriolanus had the military genius of a Tamburlaine and yet was cast out of his native city by a spiteful Roman populace, who preferred to be ignominiously weak without him rather than gloriously strong with him. In the Renaissance the monarchic form of government was generally looked upon as best, the aristocratic as faulty but next best, and the democratic as bad; and Coriolanus might readily be seen as a staunch member of a ruling aristocracy who quite properly had no love for the hydra-headed, fickle multitude of Rome. His lack of love for the common people of his city could be made into an outstanding virtue—though not, be it noted, on the authority of Plutarch.

For example, the garrulous Welshman Ludovic Lloyd, one of the sergeants-at-arms and gentlemen in ordinary to Queen Elizabeth, who fancied himself for the way in which he could work shreds of classical learning into almost any kind of discussion, saw Coriolanus in that light. In *The Consent of Time* (1590) Lloyd pictures him as a "rare man" who was banished for his virtues and who later, when he had it in his power to take revenge, spared Rome because of the compassion he felt for his family:

> In *Rome* dwelt a rare man of great seruice in the warres of *Tarquine,* whom *Largius* the first *Dictator* knewe to be such as deserued great prayse then, being a young man: for he was crowned with Oken leaues according to the *Romanes* maners in *Tarquinius* dayes, and sithence profited *Rome* in diuers seruices, in subduing the *Volscans,* in winning the citie *Corioles,* he inuaded the *Antiates,* and often repressed the insolencie of the people, insomuch that the *Romanes* hauing many warres in those dayes, this *Coriolanus* was at them all: for there was no battell fought, no warre enterprised, but *Coriolanus* returned from thence with fame and honour. But his vertue and renowme gate him much enuie: for hereby hee was banished *Rome* by the *Ediles* & *Tribunes* of the people, against the Patricians will: but the *Romanes* made a rodde to beate them selues, when they banished *Coriolanus:* for he came in armes against his owne Countrie and Citie with the *Volscans,* being at that time their generall. . . . *Volumnia* his mother, and *Virgillia* his wife with their two young sonnes gotten by *Coriolanus,* with *Valeria* the sister of *Publicolo,* and diuers other Ladies of *Rome* came to meete *Coriolanus,* to entreate for peace vnto the *Volscans* campe, and what time hee had compassion of his mother, of his wife, and of his two sonnes, and of the other Ladies being his neere kinswomen: then he withdrew his armie from *Rome,* and yeelded to the teares of his mother: but the fickle mindes of the people by the conspiracie of *Tullus Aufidius* were such, that *Coriolanus* was murdered in the Citie of *Antium,* at his very returne from that voyage.[1]

In *The Stratagems of Ierusalem* (1602) Lloyd has more to say about the high deserts of Coriolanus and the great injustice of his banishment. Here again Lloyd does not mention his faults. Coriolanus was one of the "best deserued men in *Rome*." Like Scipio Africanus, Metellus, and "diuers others of the best Romanes," he was "vniustly banished." Yet he was capable of "sparing to destroy his vngratefull countrey" because of the tears shed by his mother and his wife. For this act of mercy he was slain by the Volscians; "he might well haue said as *Scypio Affrican* said at *Linternum* after he was banished, *Ingrata patria non habebis ossa mea,* Oh vngratefull countrey, thou shalt not possesse my bones." [2] . . .

But if it was possible for the Renaissance sometimes to be blind to the faults of Coriolanus, it was also possible for it sometimes to see them as plainly as Plutarch had intended them to be seen, though in

---

[1] Pp. 496–497.
[2] Pp. 311–312.

a Christian rather than a pagan light. The haughtiness and angry impatience that Plutarch had found in Coriolanus and had attributed to faulty education could be made into instructive examples of moral failings that should be severely condemned by all followers of the Christian tradition. They could be taken as pride and wrath by an age that had by no means forgotten the spiritually destructive qualities of these two deadly sins. They could be thought of as pernicious vices or ruinous passions. In the *Politicke, Moral, and Martial Discourses, Written in French by M. Iaques Hurault . . . and translated into English by Arthur Golding* (1595) Coriolanus is named in one context as a "man of valour" who like some others of his nature had been hindered in all "well doing" by the "only vice" of pride. Plutarch is the authority quoted: "*Plutarch* in the life of *Coriolane,* saith, That the proud and stoure nature of *Coriolane,* was the cause of his ruine, notwithstanding that therwithall he was one of the absolutest men of all the Romanes. For whereas pride of it selfe is odious to all men, surely when it is matched with ambition, then becommeth it much more sauage and vntollerable." [3] In another context in the same work Coriolanus is named as a "great personage" and "but for his choler, one of the forwardest in Rome." Choler "did raigne so sore in him, that it made him of small account, and vnmeet to liue and be conuersant with men." Again Plutarch is the authority quoted: "And as the same authour [Plutarch] saith in the life of *Coriolanus,* Anger seemeth to be magnanimity, because it hath a desire to ouercome, and will not yeeld to any man: and yet for all that it is but a feeblenes, the which thrusteth the choler forth, as the weakest and most passionate part of the soule, no less than a corrupt matter of an imposthume. They that have vpheld, that cholericke persons are apt to learne, haue added that they were not fit for gouernement, and therefore that the Lacedemonians praied dayly vnto God, to inable them to beare wrongs: esteeming that person vnworthie to be in authoritie, or to deale in great affairs, that is subiect to anger." [4]

Shakespeare is so far from being blind to the faults of Coriolanus that he makes them as pernicious as any moralist of his age makes them. He gives them, with regard to their effects in this world, the destructive powers of deadly sins, and he allows them to wear the aspects of deadly sins. Outwardly the Coriolanus of Shakespeare is much like the haughty and angrily impatient Coriolanus of Plutarch, but inwardly he is a very different man; for as Coriolanus passes

[3] P. 271.
[4] Pp. 361–362.

through the hands of Shakespeare, the overlying haughtiness, the "hawtie obstinate minde," given him by Plutarch becomes an underlying pride, a spiritual flaw reaching to the depth of his being, and this deep-going pride has deep-going wrath in its train instead of mere angry impatience. Moreover, the wrath of Shakespeare's Coriolanus is much more clearly subsidiary to pride than the angry impatience of Plutarch's Coriolanus is subsidiary to haughtiness. Shakespeare's Coriolanus is often a wrathful man, but always and before all else he is a proud man. Whenever we see his wrath, we know that it is fed by pride.

The tragedy made by Shakespeare out of Plutarch's story of Coriolanus is not that of a noble spirit ruined by lack of education, which is the tragedy that Plutarch outlines. It is the tragedy of a noble spirit ruined by something in itself which education cannot touch, or at least does not touch. We do not hear anything in Shakespeare's play about the hero's lacking instruction because of his father's death and thus acquiring a faulty character. On the contrary, we learn that Volumnia, the strong-willed mother of the hero, has been both father and mother to him, has devoted herself, according to her lights, to the education of his character, and has certainly not failed to teach him how to be manly. By her precepts and her praises she has stimulated his valor. We have her own word for it that she does not approve of his unbending pride, and presumably she has done what she could to check it when she saw it standing in the way of his advancement. She is not the best of teachers to show him how to overcome his pride, but at least she can condemn it as something not drawn from her:

> Thy valiantness was mine, thou suck'dst it from me,
> But owe thy pride thyself.   (III, ii, 129–130)

The pride she condemns is what she says it is, a thing of his own, fixed in his nature. It is in the original substance of his character and is not an untutored churlishness acquired through the accident of his father's death.

But there is that about the pride of her son which Volumnia is quite incapable of understanding. Though she sees clearly that it can keep him from gaining the highest honors in Rome, she does not see that it can also keep him from base timeserving. It is more worthy of condemnation than she knows, but at the same time it is worthy of praise in a way that she does not even suspect. Her pupil shows reaches of nobility for which she is not responsible, and he shows them even in his valor, which is not a virtue of her creation, as she seems to think, but a virtue grounded in his natural pride. This valor has been developed but not called into being by her instruction.

The pride of Coriolanus has two very contradictory faculties. It is the tragic flaw in his character and therefore has the well-known power of pride, the preëminent deadly sin, to produce other faults and destroy good in the spirit of its possessor; but it is at the same time the basis of self-respect in his character and thus has power to produce good in his spirit. Whether destructive of good or productive of good, it is a fierce pride, accompanied by a wrath that makes it work at white heat. The wrath is like the pride it accompanies in not always having the qualities of a deadly sin; it can at times be righteous wrath, directed against human baseness. Hence both the pride and the wrath of Coriolanus can be admirable as well as detestable. Just as taints and honors "wage equal" with the sensualistic Antony, so do they with the proud Coriolanus. . . .

Coriolanus, then, can be thought of as greatly noble, and a chorus of Volscians urges us at the end of the tragedy to remember him thus. He is probably the last of the paradoxically noble heroes of Shakespeare's last tragic world. It is likely that few of us would call him the best of those "rare spirits" and that many would call him the worst. He is monstrously deficient as a human being, and his deficiency is the more unfortunate because it tends not to foster pity for him but to destroy any that we might give him. As a tragic hero he therefore has a marked disadvantage which is not shared by Timon, Macbeth, or Antony. Each of these others asks for our pity in a manner not to be denied—even Macbeth, who himself is pitiless but comes to know pitifully that by being pitiless he has lost "honour, love, obedience, troops of friends." Coriolanus, the fanatical lover of himself who never knows disillusionment, whose pride is so great that his spiritual self-sufficiency is never shaken, repels pity at any time, and when he does not inspire admiration, he is apt to inspire such detestation as to leave no room for pity.

As Shakespeare gives form to his last tragic world, he is always daring in his efforts to make the paradox of the deeply flawed noble hero yield subtle truth. In *Coriolanus* he pushes this paradox to its limit of tragic validity, and sometimes even beyond, with the result that he makes it more acceptable to the mind than to the heart. The deeply flawed Coriolanus who repels pity is too deeply flawed for Shakespeare's tragic purposes. Most of us who perceive nobility of spirit in him would doubtless rather praise it than associate with it.

In *Coriolanus* the problem of evil, once terribly urgent for Shakespeare, is almost completely absorbed within the dramatic hypothesis of a man who is supremely guilty of pride the vice and at the same time supremely noble in pride the virtue. Shakespeare constructs the hypothesis with mathematical precision. He uses the very greatest care to strike a balance between the repellent Coriolanus and the admirable Coriolanus, and he keeps the balance in a spirit both ironically superior and dispassionately just. The achievement, though delicately beautiful, has a quality that can only be called forbidding. About the play as a whole there is a lack of essential warmth amounting even to bleakness, and it is not for nothing that the verse is often eloquent but seldom deeply moving, often impressive but seldom sublime. *Coriolanus* is a magnificent failure in which Shakespeare seems to have brought his tragic inspiration to an end by taking tragedy into an area of paradox beyond the effective reach of merely human pity.

Coriolanus

by A. P. Rossiter

Shakespeare may have felt some disappointment with *Coriolanus*. He would not be the last; for I think that few see or read it without feeling that they "don't get as much out of it as they hoped to" or that it "somehow doesn't seem to *pay*" or is "less profitable than others I could think of"; or something like that. But whatever he thought he meant by the play is likely to be very different from what *we* make of it, unless we keep our attention fixed on what was going on inside Shakespeare's head in 1607—and what was going on in the year 1607 too. I do not mean that unless we know the barley-markets for 1606–8 and the state of malt-investments, we cannot understand *Coriolanus*. I suggest only this: that there are many ways of interpreting this play, and the one that begins nearest to Jacobean times is one that is necessarily a long way from our own. Moreover, so far as I can judge, the interpretations that arise spontaneously in our own times are so violently opposed to one another, and lead so inevitably into passionate political side-tracks, that almost any line of thinking that gets us away from them gives the play a better chance: a chance as a tragic play.

"Political": there I said it. *Coriolanus* is about power: about State, or *the* State; about order in society and the forces of disorder which threaten "that integrity which should become 't" (III. i. 159); about conflict, not in personal but political life; and—the aspect which catches our minds first?—about the conflict of classes. I put that last deliberately, for two related but separable reasons. First, if we begin at that end, the play's tragic qualities are endangered at once: it tends to be seen as political, i.e., to be filled with imported feelings which are too partisan for the kind of contemplation which is tragedy. It also readily becomes polemical and seems to be giving *answers*, solu-

"Coriolanus." *From* Angel with Horns and Other Lectures on Shakespeare by A. P. Rossiter, edited by Graham Storey (London: Longmans, Green and Co., Ltd. New York: Theatre Arts Books, 1961), pp. 235–39, 241–52. Reprinted by permission of Theatre Arts Books. The chapter has been slightly abridged for this volume.

tions to human conflicts, which tragedy does *not*. Secondly, it suffices here to summarize a few conclusions, merely as examples of "passionate political side-tracks."

1. Hazlitt: "The whole dramatic moral . . . is that those who have little shall have less, and that those who have much shall take all that others have left. The people are poor; therefore they ought to be starved. They are slaves; therefore they ought to be beaten. They work hard; therefore they ought to be treated like beasts of burden." [1] And so on. It is only necessary to read the text, to say that Hazlitt's Jacobinical comments are false and nonsensical. No question of politics arises: it is simply one of reading.

2. In December 1933, *Coriolanus* was played at the *Comédie française*. Every performance turned into a demonstration by Right-wing groups (it was the time of the Stavisky affair, and Parliamentary government itself seemed to be quite likely to come to an end); and the Royalists cheered every outburst against the "common cry of curs," the populace, and the bald tribunes whose power should be thrown in the dust. The play was withdrawn; M. Daladier dismissed the director, put the chief of the Sûreté in his place; and events went forward to the great riots of 6 February 1934.[2] While one can admire the French enthusiasm for making Shakespeare really about something that matters here and now, this is still something other than Shakespeare-criticism. For the view that Caius Marcius should be—or ever could be—the good and great dictator, the integrator of a shaking state, is one that the play cannot support for a moment. Shakespeare's source, Plutarch, had indeed said precisely the opposite; and Shakespeare has put enough into the mouth of Aufidius alone (IV. vii. 35 f.) to make further reference superfluous.

3. I have been told that the Russian view is (or was) that this is an entirely acceptable play, on the class-war; but showing how the Revolution is betrayed by self-seeking demagogues who mislead the workers for their own private ends. So that Brutus and Sicinius are wicked persons (with their modern counterparts in the Labour Party, I suppose), since the deviationist is worse than the despot. This is only what I have been told.

4. But Mr. Donald Douglas, in the *Daily Worker* (March 1952), saluted the Stratford production with the interpretation that *Coriolanus* is a revolutionary play, but one gone wrong, and patched up at the end to appease the censorship. The crack can be seen in IV. vi., when the First Citizen leads the rest astray by saying

> For mine own part,
> When I said banish him, I said 'twas pity.
> *Second Cit.:* And so did I.

[1] *Characters of Shakespeare's Plays*, 1817.
[2] See the *Manchester Guardian*, 21 March 1952, "Class War by the Avon."

> *Third Cit.:* And so did I; and, to say the truth, so did very
>   many of us;

—and it is not the Party Line at all. For the rest, let Mr. Douglas speak
for himself: "In the citizens' revolt against the Roman profiteers who
are hoarding corn against a rise in prices . . . we have the fact of
the people's power. In the banished Coriolanus, vowing destruction
on his native city . . . we have the counterpart of the modern capi-
talist determined to ruin his country if only he can destroy the people."

Those four views will do. I shall not argue with any of them,
beyond saying that, given similar latitudes of interpretation (not to
say perversion) of Shakespeare's words, I will demonstrate that Coriolanus is an allegory of more than one political idealist of our time,
who followed his own inner counsels, despised common humanity, betrayed his trust, to become a lonely dragon in a fen; and then felt
some new promptings of human nature, and threw away the game
he had given away—to end in ruin and the mystery of the darkness of
a mind that has set itself to stand

> As if a man were author of himself
> And knew no other kin.

. . . By "political" I do not mean the class-war, nor even narrowly
the Tudor system of God-ordained order. I mean *Coriolanus* plays on
political feeling: the capacity to be not only intellectually, but emotionally and purposively, engaged by the management of public affairs; the businesses of groups of men in (ordered) communities; the
contrivance or maintenance of agreement; the establishment of a
will-in-common; and all the exercises of suasion, pressure, concession
and compromise which achieve that *will* (a mind to *do*) in place of a
chaos of confused appetencies. . . .

The advantage of such an approach—"political" in the sense of the
word in Aristotle's *Politics*—is that it leads you out of any academic
or antiquarian restrictions, without landing you in the troubles which
arise from prejudices about democracy imported from the nineteenth
century or later. The terms in which the mob is described need not
worry you. "The mutable rank-scented many," "the beast with many
heads": those are Elizabethan commonplaces. The root phrase was
Horace's (*belua multorum capitum*), and that was not original; a
Stoic, Ariston of Chios, called the People πολυκέφαλον θηρίον; and
versions and variants can be found in Bacon, Chapman, Dekker,
Marston, Massinger, Middleton, Ford and (as we should expect)
Beaumont and Fletcher. To get indignant with Shakespeare for such

expressions is quixotic absurdity. He did not insult his audience, for
the simple reasons that they knew nothing of voters' vanity, and *did*
know, quite certainly, that they were *not* a mob. Yet, when I say
that, do not imagine that a man does not *mean* a "commonplace,"
merely because it is a commonplace. The many-headedness of those
expressions is, surely, a measure of Shakespeare's fear: his fear of
disorder, civil commotion, the disintegrated State. I shall return to
that point.

The other advantage of responding to political feeling in the
play is that we need not freeze it to a rigid Tudor-myth pattern of
order. That is, we need not narrow it to what it doubtless showed
to many *c.* 1607–8: an exposition of the evils which arise in the
God-ordained microcosmic State when degree is neglected; when
pride and Luciferian ambition make a great soldier into a "limb
diseased" of the body-politic; and when subjects attempt to judge
what rulers are good for them—which is (as the 33rd Homily said,
in a very convenient phrase too) "as though the foot must judge
of the head: an enterprise very heinous, and must needs breed
rebellion." That is by far the easiest way to systematize or pattern the
play. Make the Fable of the Belly the key; turn all to Tudor-political
moral allegory; throw in all the images of the body, disease, physic;
and it all comes out pat. But you will have lodged the play back in
Tudor distances, stopped all live political feeling, and set yourself the
task of imaginatively thinking about the State solely in terms which
can mean nothing whatever to your political self—unless you are
highly eccentric and an anachronism in the twentieth century.

None the less, some imaginative attempt of that kind must be made;
for the explicit political principles in the play are mainly put into
the mouth of Coriolanus; and particularly in iii. i., where he makes
what is in effect a single political utterance, though in several parts.
He says that the power of the people has increased, and must be
diminished; the Senators have nourished the cockle of rebellion by
the corn-dole: made themselves no better than plebeians to let these
Tribunes play the Senator with their "absolute 'shall'"; the people
think that concessions have been made through fear; no stable or
ordered policy can come from direction by ignorant numbers through
"voices" (votes); and the State is ruined and disintegrated unless this
power of disordering policy and vetoing wise decisions is taken away
from them. No statement of policy could be more sincere: none less
well-timed. It is Marcius's "tragic blunder" (the Aristotelian ἁμαρτία)
to state these convictions when he does. Yet so far as Shakespeare tells
us what is right for the State in the play, there we have it. We may
dislike it: we can say it belongs to a past age (and that Charles Stuart
lost his head because he did not see that that age was past); we can

say that we dislike the man who speaks (and there is no reason that I can see to *like* Coriolanus at any stage of the play). But the personality of Caius Marcius is one thing, and the convictions of Coriolanus are quite another. The rightness of a man's ideas or convictions is not affected by his unpleasantness; *or* by his popularity, his "popular 'shall.'" Indeed, being right is rarely too conducive to popularity. What is amiss with demagogy, but that it confuses popularity (what people like hearing) with rightness (expediency)? What do Brutus and Sicinius display, but just that? . . .

The personality of Caius Marcius, his attempts to manage men everywhere but on the battlefield, are, you may say, wrong throughout. But his convictions about the State are good and right, however impolitically he may phrase or time them. There you have a tragic clash: the basis of a political tragedy, not a Tudor morality. And to achieve that, Shakespeare had to twist his source, for he and Plutarch are entirely at odds. . . .

Let me take but a single example of the peculiar clashes we can feel in the person of Caius Marcius. Mainly, Shakespeare views him with detachment. And yet he has achieved an amazing imaginative triumph in the affair of the Consulship: in his penetration to the very feel and surge of patrician hauteur, in all its passionate wilfulness, its physical loathing of the rubs and smarms of the "democratic" bowling-green, where every Jack is there to be kissed by his would-be master. Do not jump to wild conclusions about my politics. Surely any man of any dignity must feel something base in the pranks that men (apparently) must employ to get the good opinion—and the vote—of other men? If so, there is a comical rightness in old Volumnia's image for the way he is to behave:

> Now humble as the ripest mulberry
> That will not hold the handling.[3]   (III. ii. 79)

It is a derogatory image, worthy of Ben Jonson; and in its context, a satiric comment on all political candidates. Is there not ethical rightness, too, in Marcius's sudden revulsion against playing the male harlot to catch votes, piping like a eunuch, smiling like a knave, and whining for a hand-out like a beggar?

> I will not do't,
> Lest I surcease to honour mine own truth,
> And by my body's action teach my mind
> A most inherent baseness.   (III. ii. 120)

He is excessive, no doubt. But if there is some truth and honourable

[3] Stratford, 1952, cut these lines. Is even Shakespeare's mulberry-tree forgotten there?

rightness there, then so much the greater the conflict: the conflict proper to a political tragedy.

I shall not analyse his character; but these few comments seem worth offering. Marcius's pride and arrogance need no examples. But the comic touch that that kind of self-greatness invites is by no means absent from the play. It is nonsense to call it a satire—as O. J. Campbell [4] did—yet throughout there are deft touches of ironical suggestion that strike the iron demi-god between the joints of the harness. The sadistic ways of Marcius junior with unamenable butterflies are neatly pointed home by his mother's "One on's father's moods" (I. iii. 66). Shakespeare is keenly interested in this terrifying man, and certainly not standing aloof to condemn his sinful pride; yet he is aware of a potential absurdity. Or, put another way, he is aware of the *precariousness* of this self-greatness. Marcius's rages totter on the edge of a line which Jonson would have pushed them over—into ridicule. And when Menenius is putting the fear of the demi-god into the Tribune Sicinius for the last time, this Jonsonian topple does occur, revealing a grotesquely comic aspect of the bogeyman which had been kept under till then:

> The tartness of his face sours ripe grapes; when he walks, he moves like an engine and the ground shrinks before his treading. He is able to pierce a corslet with his eye, talks like a knell, and his hum is a battery.   (v. iv. 17 f.)

We laugh—at the scared Tribunes, or at Menenius's *Schadenfreude*; but the comment still rebounds on Marcius. It is a queer preparation for the death of the tragic hero.

This comic irony is paralleled by the ironies of the major political scenes, where we watch great events being determined; yet watch them with some infiltration of an awareness that there is a preposterous unreasonableness about the ways in which the destinies of peoples are settled: much rather by the shortcomings and littlenesses of men than by anything great about them. It is an awareness of potential absurdity (as in the Galley-scene in *Antony and Cleopatra*). Our reaction may be only *discomfort*: it depends on one's ironic capacity. Pursue that irony—present all through Act III—and another aspect of Marcius is found: one near the heart of his tragedy. It is an irony of frustration; and when I hit on that phrase, I almost find it all prefigured in the little incident in I. ix. 79 f. when, after the battle, he asks for the life of the poor man who was his host at Corioli. Cominius, as General, gives him it at once; but what happens?

> *Lartius:* Marcius, his name?
> *Cor:*   By Jupiter, forgot!

―――――――――――
[4] *Shakespeare's Satire*, 1943. [Cf. this volume, p. 25.]

No such forgetting in Plutarch. It is Shakespeare's invention. "New-made honour doth forget men's names," he wrote in *King John*. The man's self-greatness frustrates himself, his own good aims, endangering not merely life but honour. As here.[5]

Now look at Marcius as a political force. He has had, from Volumnia's upbringing and from active life, the profoundest concern for the Roman State: not merely as conqueror, but from his feelings for law and order (*"Tu regere imperio populos Romane memento"*). But his very nature, passionate and wilful, makes it impossible for him to contrive or carry out those things which will maintain the unity of the State, that very unity he values so highly, "that integrity which should become't": the source of any man's (or any group's) power to make the State do good.

All this gives Menenius his place in the pattern: Menenius whom Shakespeare *made* from two lines in North's *Plutarch*: "certain of the pleasantest old men, and the most acceptable to the people. Of those Menenius Agrippa was he, who was sent for chief man." And that, with the fable of the Belly, is all. Shakespeare did the rest: to give his play a humorous, ironical, experienced, sensible, critical commentator; and, simultaneously, in the Roman political world, an "anti-type" and counterpoise to everything that is Marcius.

Menenius is much more than a comedian. He is "humorous" (both in the Elizabethan and our senses), but a "humorous *patrician*": a mocker, but one who can "spend my malice in my breath"; and he spends or vents it largely in irony, covering it with an air of sorely-tried moderation and good nature; so that even in rebuke, he implies that it is all really the other man's fault, for being so unreasonable (e.g., at IV. vi. 115 f.). He is a conciliator, aims at political compromise, but is not a weak old man. He handles the rebellious mob skilfully, and is apt with hecklers:

1st Cit.:   What could the belly answer?
Menenius: I will tell you;
                  If you'll bestow a small—of what you have little—
                  Patience awhile, you'st hear the belly's answer.

                                                    (I. i. 122–24)

The rhythm that Shakespeare gives those lines *is* Menenius (or one side of him). So is it earlier, when at I. i. 106 Shakespeare gives him the only belch in English blank verse: the

                        kind of smile,
        Which ne'er came from the lungs, but even thus—

[5] Stratford, 1952, cut this incident!

These touches show the politician as well as the "humorous" man. As politician Menenius is able to move with the dialectic of events. He is pliable, but like the reed in the fable; Caius Marcius is the oak. All through the central Act iii he is saying things like "Be calm, be calm"; "Well, well, no more of that" (iii. i. 115, on Coriolanus's corn-speech); "Come, enough." But his "mildly . . . calmly . . . temperately" is not the positive side of him. That comes out in his bulletin-phrase after the riot in iii. i: "This must be patch'd/ With cloth of any colour." There speaks a mind which is able to keep before itself the "political feeling," or emotion of political life, which I tried to outline to you: a mind which does not lose the great aim of integrity in the State, whatever immediate personal provocation it may encounter. Menenius is, therefore, a direct contrast to Caius Marcius, the hyper-sensitive battleship, so strangely constructed that though no weapon can harm it seriously, there is an open way to the magazine for the word "*traitor*," which blows the whole fighting-machine to ruins. Say that to Coriolanus (and the Tribunes know this), and his private honour makes him lose every thought of the integrity of the State. He becomes like Achilles in *Troilus and Cressida*:

> Imagin'd worth
> Holds in his blood such swol'n and hot discourse
> That 'twixt his mental and his active parts
> Kingdom'd Achilles in commotion rages,
> And batters down himself.   (ii. iii. 167–71)

Indeed, the Marcius-Menenius pattern repeats—in a very different tone—much of the Achilles-Ulysses pattern in that earlier play; as it also repeats the themes of power, honour and war. But Menenius is not lacking in feeling (as Ulysses is, perhaps). He is quite sincere in saying that he too would put his armour on, before Coriolanus should thus stoop to the herd. But in between comes the all-important proviso:

> but that
> The violent fit o' th' time craves it as physic
> For the whole state.   (iii. 2. 32)

That is: he would *not* put his armour on to fight the plebs. He accepts the necessity of "stooping," for an aim beyond self: beyond himself or Marcius's self.

With those few passages I have examined, you have the central significance of Menenius. His love of Marcius; his breathless tumble of words in welcoming his warrior back from victory; his pathos; his comically cruel treatment by the sentries: all those have their importance. But they do not give his main significance in the tragic pattern. To develop that further I should have to examine the other counterpart-*cum*-contrast to Menenius: Volumnia. Throughout, Caius Marcius hangs between the influence of the two. They are opposites; and the irony is that they both desire the same victory for him. Only it never could be the same: for in political life, means determine ends, and the "identical" end, won by opposite means, is quite another end.

Menenius's significance is one thread to take hold of the tragic pattern by: he is (what Marcius is not) a political mind which moves with the dialectic of events. As he can *think* (and will) *dialectically,* he remains true to the major loyalties: Rome and himself. Marcius, the man of "principle," does not. In this play, Bradley's generalization is entirely true: "To meet these circumstances something is required which a smaller man might have given, but which the hero cannot give." [6] Thus Marcius's "greatness" is fatal to him. But *is* it great? I do not propose to answer that: only to insist that the comic ironies of the action (and phrasing) push the question at us; and that reflection offers the paradox that Menenius is "greater" in mind than Marcius.

The valuation of Marcius is, however, offered by Shakespeare himself: in Aufidius's speech at the end of Act IV (IV. vii. 35 f.), a speech which perplexed Coleridge utterly.[7] It is, as he rightly says, "out of character"; but in it Shakespeare sums up Marcius. He was first "a noble servant" to Rome; but whether from pride, or defect of judgement, or unadaptable rigidity of nature (which made him attempt to manage peace as he did war)—and he had "spices" of all these— he came to be feared, hated and banished. That he epitomizes any of these faults is explicitly denied. But two of them particularly concern what I used Menenius to focus: the qualities of a political mind, able to remain effective in a changing world of events. Whatever pride may be, rigidity (however high-principled) and "defect of judgement" are the opposites of those qualities. But Aufidius (and Shakespeare) adds:

> So our virtues
> Lie in th' interpretation of the time.

Now that, in one and a half lines, gives the essence of the play. Run over the whole action, act by act, and each is seen as an "estimate" or valuation of Marcius: enemy of the people—demi-god of war—

---

[6] *Shakespearean Tragedy*, p. 21.

[7] *Lectures on Shakespeare*, 1818. Coleridge cherished the hope that he would become wiser, and discover some profound excellence in what he could only see as an imperfection; but I think he could never see it except as "out of character."

popular hero home in triumph—consul-elect—and then (through
his assertion of what he always *had* asserted) public enemy and
banished man, "a lonely dragon" (IV. i. 30). Throughout all this, he
himself is almost an absolute *constant*. Then, on his way to Aufidius
at Antium, we have his one soliloquy:

> O world, thy slippery turns! Friends now fast sworn,
> Whose double bosoms seem to wear one heart,
> Whose hours, whose bed, whose meal and exercise
> Are still together, who twin, as 'twere, in love
> Unseparable, shall within this hour,
> On a dissension of a doit, break out
> To bitterest enmity.   (IV. iv. 12 f.)

It is strangely reminiscent of the sad midnight reflections of Henry
IV, looking back over Richard's time; yes, and thinking about history.
But what is Marcius's speech about, if not that same world of history,
where all is change, nothing absolute; where all "virtues" lie in the
interpretation of the time, and all times lie about the virtues they
have lost the use for?

This is very near to what Ulysses tells Achilles about Time's
wallet and the "one touch of nature" that "makes the whole world
kin." The "touch" is an incessant writing-off of past values, an
interminable revaluation-series. This is what happens in the historical
process: history always *goes on*; goes on, if you like, to the sad and
cynical tune of *Frankie and Johnnie*:

> This story has no moral,
> This story has no end,
> This story only goes to show
> That there ain't no good in men . . .

Or shall we say, "There is not enough good of an effective kind,
in men as they appear in the historical process"? Be that as it may,
this is what happens in that process. History always goes on; and in
this play even Bradley could not say that re-established order and
rightness are left to console us. There is no Albany; not even a
Fortinbras or a Malcolm; the survivor is Tullus Aufidius.

Coriolanus is the last and greatest of the Histories. It is Shakespeare's only great political play; and it is slightly depressing, and
hard to come to terms with, because it is *political tragedy*. The idea
of the State runs through it:

> the Roman state; whose course will on
> The way it takes, cracking ten thousand curbs . . .
>   (I. i. 67)

And ten thousand men. Yet it is *not* the ideal or cosmic state of
the other plays: rather, an abstraction from an organism, or a real
state. Real states are dynamic: hence the constant irony in the play,
especially of Marcius and Aufidius saying what they *will* do, and
then not doing it or doing it in a way that neither had foreseen.[8]
Hence too the changing valuations of the same Marcius by Aufidius,
or by the comic servants in Antium, who snub him muffled and
then say they knew all along he was Somebody. This re-estimation
of Marcius goes on to the bitter end: to Aufidius's stepping off his
stabbed body—"My rage is gone"—and calling for a hero's funeral.
"O world, thy slippery turns!"

But, in a sense, Caius Marcius *Coriolanus* was dead already. That
fine speech which Shakespeare made by transforming North—

> My name is Caius Marcius, who hath done
> To thee particularly, and to all the Volsces,
> Great hurt and mischief   (IV. v. 65 f.):

what is it but the equivalent of a *dying*-speech, a summary of expir-
ing greatness? "Only that name remains" is no more than truth: he
is no more *Coriolanus*—as Aufidius will tell him, before he stabs him.

The final depressing paradox is that Marcius's unyieldingness and
would-be self-sufficiency make him so pliant to force of circumstance.
All told, he is as unstable and trustless as those whom he abused with:

> you are no surer, no,
> Than is the coal of fire upon the ice
> Or hailstone in the sun . . .
> . . . . . . and your affections are
> A sick man's appetite . . .   (I. i. 170 f.)

Shakespeare spares him that last twist of bitter reflection: the words
were spoken to the mob. But the reflection is there, in the play. And
on my view, it ends—as J. W. N. Sullivan says that Beethoven's

[8] Examples are Marcius's statements about what he will do to Aufidius:
> Were half to half the world by th'ears, and he
> Upon my party, I'd revolt, to make
> Only my wars with him 2 (I. i. 231–23);

and
> At Antium lives he? . . .
> I wish I had a cause to seek him there,
> To oppose his hatred fully (III. i. 18–20).

Others are: Aufidius's early threat to murder Marcius "were it/At home . . . even
there/Against the hospital canon" (I. i. 24–26); and Marcius's assurance to his
mother, as he leaves Rome in exile, that he "Will or exceed the common or be
caught/With cautelous baits and practice" (IV. i. 32–33). Here the irony is double:
both things happen, but in no foreseeable sense.

Coriolan ends—"in utter darkness": the darkness of history, from which Shakespeare finally absconded—with *Cymbeline*. I cannot accept Bradley's hint to make this the bridge-head towards the Romances: but I rejoice to concur with Mr. Eliot: *one of* Shakespeare's most assured artistic successes—as perfect in control as *1 Henry IV*.

The Dramatic Use of Imagery
in Shakespeare's *Coriolanus*

by Maurice Charney

Coriolanus is the last of Shakespeare's tragedies and it is also
the one perhaps least often discussed or performed. In contrast
with *Antony and Cleopatra* of a year or so earlier,[1] it seems a fairly
cold and unpoetic work and suggests an exhaustion of Shakespeare's
powers after a period of great tragedies. With the exception of such
critics as Granville-Barker and G. Wilson Knight, this interpretation
of *Coriolanus* has been the dominant one. The ordinary criteria of
richness of imagery, complexity of thought, and penetrating character
analysis do not seem to apply here. Yet from a dramatic point of view,
the play has a surprising force and vitality. It uses a difficult two-
part form that succeeds where *Julius Caesar* fails, for by a series of
mounting climaxes it reaches the high point of Coriolanus' yielding
in V, iii, whereas *Julius Caesar* seems to fall apart after the murder
of Caesar in the third act. There is also a masterful handling of mob
scenes in *Coriolanus*, and these emphasize the thoroughly political
tone of the tragedy. In this context, the sparseness of verbal imagery
and imaginative effects give the impression of a lean vigor—a kind
of classical perfection of form.

The recent production of *Coriolanus* at the Phoenix Theater[2] seems
to justify the otherwise bewildering remark of Eliot that this play
is, "with *Antony and Cleopatra*, Shakespeare's most assured artistic

"The Dramatic Use of Imagery in Shakespeare's Coriolanus*" by Maurice Charney.
From ELH 23 (1956): 183–93. © 1956 by The Johns Hopkins Press. Reprinted by
permission of The Johns Hopkins Press. A considerably expanded version of this
essay appears as "The Imagery of* Coriolanus*" in* Shakespeare's Roman Plays: The
Function of Imagery in Drama *by Maurice Charney (Cambridge, Mass.: Harvard
University Press, 1961), pp. 142–97.*

[1] E. K. Chambers, *William Shakespeare*, Oxford, 1930, I, 479–80. Chambers thinks
Coriolanus may have been produced early in 1608.

[2] This production was directed by John Houseman and opened on January 19,
1954 at the Phoenix Theater in New York City ("Coriolanus," *New York Theatre
Critics' Review: 1954*, XV (Jan. 25, 1954), 385–88).

success." [3] We need to adjust our criticism to the fact that the language of the play is almost a subordinate factor in its effect. Thus a literal analysis of the verbal imagery would not prove very rewarding, for the images are not so much valuable for themselves as for the dramatic uses to which they are put. We also need to extend our concept of "image" beyond the mere words of the play to the actual performance in the theater. Costume, stage properties, gesture, grouping, and the theater itself all provide us with significant images. This is the gap that separates a reading from an actual performance, and in *Coriolanus,* particularly, this "presented" or "presentational" imagery lies at the heart of the imaginative experience of the play.

The character of the imagery in *Coriolanus* is closely linked to the character of the protagonist. As A. C. Bradley said of him, "If Lear's thunder-storm had beat upon his head, he would merely have set his teeth." [4] Coriolanus is an unreflective man of action, and this makes his tragedy massive and overwhelming—almost like fate —but this also keeps it from touching us very personally. Neither Coriolanus nor any of the characters in this play are either inward or meditative or lyric, and there is not much self-awareness or tragic "recognition." Actually, only Menenius uses figurative language freely and naturally, as in the fable of the belly and the members, but his role is limited to conciliator. In this context, a rich verbal imagery would defeat the dramatic purpose, while in such a play as *Richard II* it is just this rich vein of poetic fancy that calls attention to the ineffectual and histrionic nature of the king.

When Coriolanus does use figures of speech, he inclines to similes rather than metaphors, since they provide a simpler and more explicit form of expression. Both the vehicle and tenor[5] of the image are very carefully balanced and limited, usually by the connectives "like" or "as." Thus the similes in the play do not suggest new areas of meaning, but give points already stated an added force and vividness. Their function is illustrative rather than expressive. In this respect *Coriolanus* resembles Shakespeare's early work, for the mature plays move away from the simile form towards a highly complex use of metaphor.[6] But this type of metaphor would be inappropriate to the theme and tone of *Coriolanus.*

[3] T. S. Eliot, "Hamlet," in *Selected Essays 1917–1933* (New York, 1932), p. 124.

[4] A. C. Bradley, "Coriolanus," *Proceedings of the British Academy: 1911–1912,* V, 459.

[5] See I. A. Richards, *The Philosophy of Rhetoric,* New York, 1936. The simplest definition is that the tenor is "the underlying idea or principal subject which the vehicle or figure means" (p. 97).

[6] See Wolfgang H. Clemen, *The Development of Shakespeare's Imagery,* London, 1951, e. g., p. 5.

There is a good example of the illustrative use of simile when Volumnia instructs her son in his role before the people:

> Now humble as the ripest mulberry
> That will not hold the handling—say to them
> Thou art their soldier . . .[7]   (3. 2. 79–81)

Notice the progression here of statement and illustration. Coriolanus must be "humble" before the people, and the simile emphasizes the kind of humility that is expected: "as the ripest mulberry / That will not hold the handling. . . ." Volumnia could have said: "Now humbly say to them thou art their soldier" and have made perfectly good sense. Although the mulberry simile makes a vivid illustration, it is not indispensable to the meaning of the passage in which it occurs. But Antony's simile: "indistinct / As water is in water" (*Antony and Cleopatra* 4. 14. 10–11), or Cleopatra's final similes: "As sweet as balm, as soft as air, as gentle—" (*Antony and Cleopatra* 5. 2. 314) are themselves the meaning of the passages in which they occur—they are not in any way dispensable.

This sensitive image of the "ripest mulberry" has an important dramatic function. Its highly imaginative character suggests a false tone in what Volumnia is saying. In its context, the image is overwrought, for Volumnia knows her son cannot feign any sort of humility, no less the supreme humility of the "ripest mulberry." It is too self-conscious and lush an image, and hints that there is a servile, dishonorable aspect in what Volumnia is proposing. The point in question here is a significant one for understanding the function of poetic language in the drama. If this mulberry image appeared in a poetic anthology it might seem an apt and original conceit, but in the play its effect is insidious. This is the essence of dramatic functionalism, for Shakespeare uses the poetic character of the image to indicate the maternal cajolery by which Volumnia achieves her ends.

Another example of this principle is in Coriolanus' injunction against flattery in I, ix:

> When drums and trumpets shall
> I' th' field prove flatterers, let courts and cities be
> Made all of false-fac'd soothing! When steel grows
> Soft as the parasite's silk, let him be made
> An overture[8] for th' wars!   (1. 9. 42–46)

---

[7] All quotations from Shakespeare are from George Lyman Kittredge's edition, *The Complete Works of Shakespeare*, Boston, 1936.

[8] Kittredge, following Tyrwhitt, emends the Folio reading "Ouerture" to "coverture." A. E. Thiselton clears up the difficulty of the Folio text by regarding "him"

In this overturning of order that flattery brings, the steel of the soldier (probably his mail coat) will become as soft as the silk of the parasite. It is a vivid contrast of textures, but its imaginative tone is used to suggest the luxury of peace—as if one would expect the silk-clad parasite at court to use similes, but not the steel-coated man of war. Imagination is not the practical soldier's concern. And Coriolanus prevents any possible flattery of his wounds by calling them "Scratches with briers, / Scars to move laughter only" (3. 3. 51–52). These images of peace and civil life put an unexpected music into Coriolanus' verse, although he uses them contemptuously.

There are a few places in the play where the style is deliberately heightened to achieve a dramatic effect. At the climax of V, iii, for example, Coriolanus' couplet and half-line come as a sudden change of tone:

> Not of a woman's tenderness to be
> Requires nor child nor woman's face to see.
> I have sat too long.   (5. 3. 129–31)

The couplet itself indicates the "woman's tenderness" that is growing in Coriolanus. If he did indeed want "nothing of a god but eternity and a heaven to throne in" (5. 4. 25–26), he could not speak in this way. Tenderness is not the attribute of the warrior, and the infrequency of this tone underlines its dramatic significance: the pardon for Rome is being made inevitable in the texture of the verse itself.

Coriolanus' own attitude to words helps to shape the character of the verbal imagery in the play. Suspecting he will have the worst of it, he refuses to parry arguments with the Tribune Brutus, for "oft, / When blows have made me stay, I fled from words" (2. 2. 75–76). Unlike Hamlet or Richard II or even Othello, Coriolanus has a natural antipathy to eloquence. As Menenius tells the patricians, Coriolanus' aversion to words is part of his hatred of flattery: "His heart's his mouth; / What his breast forges, that his tongue must vent . . ." (3. 1. 257–58). He is "ill-school'd / In bolted language . . ." and "meal and bran together / He throws without distinction" (3. 1. 321–23). There is no subtlety in this man, no use of language as an exploration of consciousness. He says what he thinks and feels and that is the end of it, for words are simply a means to express his bluff honesty. Remember Antony's ironic claim at the height of his oration: "I am no orator, as Brutus is . . ." (*Julius Caesar*

---

as the dative instead of the objective case. Coriolanus would then be making a scornful overture to the parasite to fight in the wars (*The Tragedie of Coriolanus,* ed. Horace Howard Furness, Jr., Philadelphia, 1928, A New Variorum edition, Vol. XX, 145–58, esp. 157).

3. 2. 222). Coriolanus is emphatically "no orator," and in a play
so thoroughly political as this, the inability to make speeches is a
claim to integrity.

Coriolanus is also peculiarly oppressed by the reality of words,
and the fluent Tribunes and Aufidius turn this weakness to their own
ends. In III, i, for example, Coriolanus seizes upon the humble
"shall" as if it were a menacing entity:

> *Sic.*   It is a mind
> That shall remain a poison where it is,
> Not poison any further.
> *Cor.*   Shall remain?
> Hear you this Triton of the minnows? Mark you
> His absolute "shall"?
> *Com.*   'Twas from the canon.
> *Cor.*   "Shall"?   (3. 1. 86–90)

And Coriolanus continues to rage against the "peremptory 'shall' "
(3. 1. 94), the "popular 'shall,' " (3. 1. 106), which is made to
symbolize the whole patrician-plebeian conflict. In terms of the actual
situation, Coriolanus' rage is excessive and strident; he is "fleeing
from words" (2. 2. 76) rather than realities. Aufidius uses the same
trick as the Tribunes in V, vi, where he tempts Coriolanus to his
doom with three contemptuous words: "traitor," "Marcius," and
"boy." Coriolanus recoils from the verbal concussion and repeats the
words unbelievingly as if they had power over him, as in his final
speech:

> Boy? False hound!
> If you have writ your annals true, 'tis there,
> That, like an eagle in a dovecote, I
> Flutter'd your Volscians in Corioli;
> Alone I did it. Boy?   (5. 6. 112–16)

For the moment, the word and the thing are confounded, produc-
ing a situation that can be resolved only by violence.

Coriolanus' normal speaking voice is often harsh and vituperative.
In his tirades against the people, he uses many repeated image
themes (e.g., food, disease, and animals), but our interest is not
so much in the images themselves as in their expletive force. After
the Romans are beaten to their trenches by the Volscians, for example,
"Enter *Marcius,* cursing" (1. 4. 29 S. D.), and his volley of abuse
begins:

> All the contagion of the South light on you,
> You shames of Rome! you herd of—⁹ Biles and plagues
> Plaster you o'er, that you may be abhorr'd
> Farther than seen and one infect another
> Against the wind a mile! You souls of geese
> That bear the shapes of men, how have you run
> From slaves that apes would beat! Pluto and hell!
>
> (1. 4. 30–36)

What is important is not the catalogue of disease and animal imagery, but the "thunder-like percussion" (1. 4. 59) of Marcius' wrath. The breaking off in "you herd of—" is not felt as a gap, but as part of a natural rhythm in which the histrionic stress is on sound rather than sense. These images are "illustrative" because they are used as examples of Marcius' wrath, and no single image nor the sequence of the group is indispensable. We do not feel any breadth of meaning here; but we must remember that it is Marcius who is speaking, and he is neither a poet nor a politician, but only a straightforward man of war. He tags plebeian faults with what is for him a suitable imagery, and if it seems familiar and trite, that in itself is a comment on his own image-making powers.

It is significant, too, that *Coriolanus* has only thirty-six lines of soliloquy: the same number as *As You Like It* and the fewest in the Shakespeare canon.¹⁰ This does not prove anything by itself, but it keeps us aware of the lack of inwardness in the play, and the fact that Coriolanus is the least articulate of Shakespeare's tragic heroes. At an opposite pole is the brooding, meditative Hamlet, who resorts to the soliloquy as a "natural" form of expression—the soliloquy in that play is a vital part of its meaning.¹¹ What soliloquies there are in *Coriolanus*, however, are used for a special dramatic effect. In a play so full of politics as this, it is not often that we see a lone figure on stage speaking as if to himself. We have been accustomed to seeing troops moving about and crowds of plebeians and patricians wrangling with each other. In this context, the soliloquy becomes a literal stage image of isolation. The two soliloquies in IV, iv, for example, emphasize the spiritual isolation of Coriolanus as an exile and traitor in the country of the Volscians, and in II, iii, Coriolanus' proud soliloquy in the gown of humility sets him completely apart from his plebeian petitioners. The stage situation of the soliloquy

⁹ The dash first appeared in Dr. Johnson's edition. The Folio reading is: "You Shames of Rome: you Heard of Byles and Plagues" (*Variorum Coriolanus*, Vol. XX, 104–07, esp. 104).

¹⁰ Morris Le Roy Arnold, *The Soliloquies of Shakespeare*, New York, 1911, p. 25.

¹¹ Arnold (*Ibid.*) counts 14 soliloquies of 291 lines in *Hamlet*.

serves as a metaphor for his inward state. He speaks to himself on
stage not to unburden his conscience or express his inner purpose,
but because he actually is at that point an asocial, tormented figure.
We have been trying to show that *Coriolanus* does not represent
a sudden artistic lapse on Shakespeare's part. Although the verbal
imagery in this play echoes Shakespeare's earlier work in its use of
the simile form, the images themselves serve a dramatic function
quite different from the rhetorical eloquence of the early plays. That
is why a strictly verbal analysis of the play's imagery cannot produce
very rewarding results. The imaginative force of *Coriolanus* lies in
that large area of non-verbal and characteristically dramatic images
that are directly presented to us in the theater.

Notice, for example, how the imagery of costume expresses the
dramatic meaning. We have perhaps lost some of the Elizabethan
idea of dress as an indication of a man's place in society and way
of life,[12] but its significance is still quite clear. When Coriolanus
appears in the gown of humility in II, iii, there is an immediate
shock to see the aristocrat wearing humble dress. This point is
established as soon as the character walks on stage, for his costume
is a violation of social decorum. Coriolanus must perform this ceremony in order to be consul, but he does it unwillingly and with
heavy mockery. There is a real discordance between his inner hatred
of the people and his outward signs of humility. Costume is used
ironically to show that Coriolanus is not the man he seems: he is
merely dressed humbly, but not humble in spirit. There is a physical
uncomfortableness in wearing the gown that approaches a moral
state, and it is up to the actor to convey this discomfort by the
proper gesture and stage business. Coriolanus himself is as much
isolated from the gown he wears as from his plebeian petitioners.
The basis of the imagery here lies in the visual effect of the costume,
and the verbal images of "The napless vesture of humility" (2. 1. 250)
and "this wolvish toge" (2. 3. 122) support what we actually see on
the stage.

Costume is used again as an important dramatic symbol in IV, iv,
where the exiled Coriolanus appears at the house of his former enemy,
Aufidius. The opening stage direction of the scene sets the tone
for Coriolanus' banishment: "Enter *Coriolanus* in mean apparel,
disguis'd and muffled." This image, too, comes as a sudden shock. We
have not seen Coriolanus since his departure from Rome in IV, i, and
he now appears entirely changed from the heroic figure of the first
part of the play. His spiritual isolation is translated into the theatrical
terms of "mean apparel, disguis'd and muffled." The imagery of

[12] See M. Channing Linthicum, *Costume in the Drama of Shakespeare and his
Contemporaries*, Oxford, 1936.

costume provides a convenient shorthand symbolism for what might
require pages of background explanation in the novel. Thus Shakespeare is able to jump boldly and without transition from Coriolanus
in Rome to Coriolanus in Antium. While the gown of humility in
II, iii expressed a false humbleness put on unwillingly, this "mean
apparel" represents a true humbling of circumstance—this is the
low point to which Coriolanus has fallen. In both scenes, the in-
appropriateness of the costume for the character of the hero is what
is important, and the constraint and uncomfortableness of it must
be emphasized in the acting.

In these scenes in Act Four, the feast of Aufidius off-stage also
isolates the ill-clad, somber Coriolanus: he is out of place in these
surroundings. We never actually see this feast, but we are kept
aware of it by the bustle of servants carrying food and drink and by
the sounds of music and revelry coming from within. It is good
dramatic economy to keep this feast off-stage, since it only serves
as a background for the appearance of Coriolanus. As in the off-stage
sounds of battle in *Antony and Cleopatra* (4. 12. 9 S. D.) and the
shoutings of the mob in *Julius Caesar* (1. 2. 78 S. D., 1. 2. 131 S. D.),
Shakespeare makes effective use of "sound effects." This imagery of
sound may be more suggestive than a comparable visual imagery
and it reaches a kind of perfection in the "Music of the hautboys . . .
under the stage" in *Antony and Cleopatra* (4. 3. 11 S. D.) and in the
"noises" of *The Tempest*. It is just this type of imagery that is most
difficult for a reader of plays to appreciate, since the actual music
or sounds of the play are only indicated by stage directions and
allusions in the printed text.

Another significant presentational theme is the imagery of silence[13]
in V, iii. This imagery develops the climax of the play from
Coriolanus' inflexible resolution to the breaking of his pride. Consider the actual stage situation. Coriolanus is silent from his two
lines at line 92 to the couplet and half-line at line 129, and from
this point until his mercy speech more than fifty lines further (from
lines 131 to 182). In other words, Coriolanus speaks only about four
and a half of these ninety crucial lines. His silence is an image of
the isolation that is about to be destroyed from within, and is thus
perhaps more difficult to act than any of his speaking part. The
actor must not only be able to present the tense inner conflict, but
also be able to register the effect of the family appeal. He may
use any number of histrionic means, e.g., an expressionless inflex-
ibility in which the slightest movement is a sign of emotion, or an
abortive moving toward the family group then away as if to exit

[13] See Harley Granville-Barker, *Prefaces to Shakespeare,* Princeton, 1946–47, Vol.
II, esp. 155, 262, 268, and 291–92.

(but the family group hedge him in and prevent this). These are the cracks in the god-like mask of Coriolanus through which we see the human figure within.

The final acting out of the imagery of silence comes at the climax of the play. Volumnia has been speaking compulsively, as if to fill the void of her son's silence, but finally, she, too, has no more to say and makes ready to leave: "I am hush'd until our city be afire. / And then I'll speak a little" (5. 3. 181–82). At this point occurs one of those marvelous bits of staging by which Shakespeare could create a great climax: *"He holds her by the hand, silent"* (5. 3. 182 S. D.). This is the yielding of Coriolanus presented in the symbolic language of dumb-show or pantomime. The silence continues, but it is now the sign of mercy rather than inscrutable hardness. All of Shakespeare's other tragic heroes are endowed with a special eloquence at the height of their tragedies, but Coriolanus expresses himself best in the eloquence of action, and this seems completely appropriate for him. This is the climax of the play, and the words that follow only express his own wonder at what has happened:

> O mother, mother!
> What have you done? Behold, the heavens do ope,
> The gods look down, and this unnatural scene
> They laugh at.   (5. 3. 182–85)

The actual yielding of Coriolanus is marked by a simple bit of stage action: *"He holds her by the hand. . . ."* His fearful isolation has been broken, and the lone antagonistic figure who seemed by his silence to reject his family's appeal, now holds his mother's hand. Except for the kiss to Virgilia earlier in the scene (5. 3. 44–48), this is the only physical contact between Coriolanus and another human being in the entire play, and it indicates a climactic moment of reconciliation. He is tragically reunited with the forces of "Great Nature" (5. 3. 33). Compare the reconciliation of King Lear and Cordelia: he kneels to his daughter and fumblingly touches her eyes ("Be your tears wet? Yes, faith. I pray weep not." *King Lear* 4. 7. 71). Since boy actors played the women's roles on the Elizabethan stage, the playwrights of the time tended to avoid these physical contacts except at critical moments. The sparing use of this type of stage action thus gives it a special significance.

One may of course argue that what we have called "presentational" images are not images at all in the ordinary sense of the term. But in the drama an image may be something uniquely different from an image in lyric poetry or the novel. The text of a play is in some sense only the potential play that must be "realized" in performance, just as the musical score is only a notation for instrumentalists. The analogy is perhaps too extreme, but we need to bridge the logical gap between the written play and the play as performed. Because Shakespeare has become a literary institution, there is a special need to restore the fullness of meaning his plays may have in the theater. Over the lapse of three hundred and fifty years we tend to forget how closely Shakespeare was connected with the stage, not only as a playwright, but also as an actor, theater owner, and theater manager. He wrote chiefly for his own playhouse and company, and, from all indications, his plays seem to have been a great success. But the myth of Shakespeare the poet debasing himself for the stage is too deeply rooted to be dispelled. Actually, most theatergoers never bother to read the texts of the plays they see, but with Shakespeare and the "classics" it is just the opposite: we read the plays and stay at home.

Coriolanus is a case in point. Its reputation has suffered because it is not a "literary" play, and its remarkable dramatic force and vitality have been obscured. Whether or not we consider it as an anticlimax after *Antony and Cleopatra* depends upon our point of view. In this paper we have tried to look at the sparseness of imagery and the seemingly cold and unpoetic tone of *Coriolanus* in terms of dramatic needs and functions. We have thus assumed a fairly comprehensive role for imagery in the drama, one that goes beyond figures of speech and verbal references. Language in this play is only one source of imagery, and it is used not for its own sake but for specifically dramatic ends. The most significant images, however, are those that are directly presented in the theater, such details as costume, sound effects, physical contacts, and silence. It is in this area that the distinct originality and mastery of *Coriolanus* lie. The interpretation we have been suggesting puts a burden on the reader of plays to be his own actor, producer, and stage manager, and to be able to create, by the exercise of his "histrionic sensibility," [14] his own ideal performance in the theater.

[14] Francis Fergusson, *The Idea of a Theater*, Princeton, 1949, pp. 236-40.

An Interpretation of Shakespeare's *Coriolanus*

by *Charles K. Hofling, M.D.*

To a degree probably unparalleled in Shakespeare, the interest
in the play centers in the character of its hero. Coriolanus is portrayed
as a man of outstanding physical courage and valor, a man of great
aristocratic pride and arrogance, and a man of great honesty. He
is primarily a man of action, although he can be eloquent at
times. . . .

Speaking from the standpoint of psychiatric diagnosis, one would
say that the category into which Coriolanus most nearly fits is that of
phallic-narcissistic character, as originally delineated by Reich.[1] In
fact three-fourths of Reich's description applies so closely as to seem
that it could have been written about Coriolanus. A few sentences
from the first portion of this description will illustrate the point.

> . . . the typical phallic-narcissistic character is self-confident, often
> arrogant, elastic, vigorous and often impressive. . . . they most fre-
> quently belong to Kretchmer's athletic type. . . . Everyday behavior
> is . . . usually haughty, . . . derisively aggressive. . . . The outspoken
> types tend to achieve leading positions in life and resent subordination.
> . . . In contrast to other characters, their narcissism expresses itself not
> in an infantile manner but in the exaggerated display of self-confi-
> dence, dignity and superiority. . . . In spite of their narcissistic pre-
> occupation with their selves they often show strong attachments to peo-
> ple and things outside. In this respect, they resemble most closely the
> genital character; they differ from it, however, in that their actions are
> much more intensively and extensively determined by irrational mo-
> tives. It is not by accident that this type is most frequently found among
> athletes, aviators, soldiers and engineers. One of their most important
> traits is aggressive courage.

"An Interpretation of Shakespeare's Coriolanus*" by Charles K. Hofling, M.D.
From* American Imago *14 (Spring 1957): 411-31. Copyright 1957 by* American
Imago. *Reprinted by permission of the publisher. This essay has been slightly
abridged for this volume.*

[1] Reich, W. *Character Analysis* (New York: Orgone Institute Press, 1949).

The possibility for strong attachments to others is of great interest in the character of Coriolanus and of crucial importance to the drama. Leaving aside for the moment the matter of his relationship to his mother, one may say that Coriolanus has sincere and affectionate object-relationships with a number of persons: with his comrades-in-arms, Cominius and Lartius, with old Menenius, with his son, young Marcius, and, above all, with his wife, Virgilia. Perhaps the best evidence as to the nature of Coriolanus's feeling toward his wife which is afforded us prior to Act V is his first sentence of greeting to her on his return to Rome after the victory at Corioli.

> *Cor.* My gracious silence, hail!

The imaginative tenderness of this line is most revealing, not only of a strong affection, but of a considerable ability to see and react to Virgilia as she is. The line is devoid of pride and selfishness.

Having briefly considered the personality of Coriolanus as it is presented in the early portions of the drama, one is faced with several questions. How did it become what it is at the outset? To what extent is the action of the play explicable in terms of personality? Are there any changes in the personality as a result of the events of the play?

In similar situations of literary criticism one can often develop satisfactory answers to the two latter questions, but *Coriolanus* is unusual for a Shakespearean play in the extent to which the author has provided material relevant to answering the first question as well. This material consists largely in the portrayal of Volumnia, the mother of Coriolanus, and in unmistakable hints as to the history of this mother-son relationship.

It is interesting to note that Volumnia is not infrequently referred to in Shakespearean criticism in terms of considerable admiration.[2] She is supposed to typify the noble Roman matron of the days when the republic was young. A careful reading of the play falls short of substantiating this concept. It does reveal that Shakespeare regarded Volumnia as having exerted a definitely traumatic influence upon Coriolanus.

Volumnia is first introduced in Act I, Scene III. Her long initial speech affords a basis for considerable insight into her personality.

> *Vol.* I pray you, daughter, sing; or express yourself in a more comfortable sort. If my son were my husband, I should freelier rejoice in that absence wherein he won honor than in all the embracements of his bed where he would show most love. When yet he was but tender-bodied and the only son of my womb, when youth with comeliness

---

[2] Mackenzie, A. M., *The Women in Shakespeare's Plays* (New York: Doubleday, Page & Co., 1924).

plucked all gaze his way, when for a day of kings' entreaties a mother
should not sell him an hour from her beholding, I, considering how
honor would become a person, that it was no better than picture-like
to hang by th' wall, if renown made it not stir, was pleased to let him
seek danger where he was like to find fame. To a cruel war I sent him;
from whence he returned, his brows bound in oak. I tell thee, daughter,
I sprang not more in joy at first hearing he was a man-child than now
in first seeing he had proved himself a man.

Goddard says discerningly of Volumnia: ". . . she had been little
other than an Amazon, a woman—to call her that—who so rejoiced in
battle and military glory that for her vicarious satisfaction she pushed
her son into blood-shed almost before he had ceased to be a child.
She fairly feasted on wounds and scars. A wolf is said to have suckled
Romulus and Remus. Coriolanus did not need any such nourishment.
He had its human equivalent." [3] Volumnia thus is seen to be an extremely unfeminine, non-maternal person, one who sought to mold
her son to fit a preconceived image gratifying her own masculine
(actually pseudo-masculine) strivings. Her method, we learn from the
above and from other speeches, was to withhold praise and the scant
affection she had to give from any achievements except aggressive and
exhibitionistic ones.

Volumnia gives much lip-service to "honor," but this attitude proves
to be in part hypocritical. During the political crisis of Acts II and
III, she urges her son to adopt craft and dissembling until he has won
power. In other words, this woman is much more concerned about
appearances than about honor or truth as things in themselves.

The influence of Volumnia's personality on that of her son is indicated to have been the more intense by reason of the facts that
Coriolanus lost his father in infancy and, so far as we are told in
the play, had no brothers or sisters. Thus, on the one hand, the
boy's emotional needs had no source of satisfaction save this militant
mother, and, on the other, there was no guiding influence to counter-
balance hers.

The latter portion of the scene from which Volumnia's long speech
has been quoted is of crucial importance in estimating the effects of
the mother-son relationship. In the middle of the scene the Lady
Valeria is introduced. Along with Virgilia, she serves the purpose of
throwing Volumnia into contrast and showing that the latter is not
merely the typical Roman matron of the period. She does more than
this, however. She inquires about Coriolanus's son, little Marcius, and
thus gives the audience a glimpse into the hero's own childhood.

[3] Goddard, H. C., *The Meaning of Shakespeare* (Chicago: The University of
Chicago Press, 1951).

Val.   . .| How does your little son?

Vir.   I thank your ladyship; well, good madam.

Vol.   He had rather see the sword and hear a drum than look upon his
         schoolmaster.

Val.   O' my word, the father's son: I'll swear, 'tis a very pretty boy.
         O' my troth, I looked upon him o' Wednesday half an hour together;
         has such a confirmed countenance. I saw him run after a gilded butter-
         fly; and when he caught it, he let it go again; and after it again; and
         over and over he comes, and up again; catched it again; or whether
         his fall enraged him, or how 't was, he did so set his teeth and tear it.
         O, I warrant how he mammocked it!

Vol.   One on's father's moods. . . .

Vir.   A crack, madam.

Coming immediately after the passage in which Volumnia has
spoken of Coriolanus's grace and comeliness as a child and of the
standards she imposed upon him, this little vignette can only mean
that Volumnia is attempting to repeat the process with her grand-
son, and that, in effect, the little boy can be taken to represent Coriolanus, himself, at a similar age. The butterfly incident shows childish
curiosity, affection, and desire for mastery turning into sadism.

With consummate art Shakespeare reintroduces the butterfly theme
in Act IV, Scene VI. Cominius and Menenius are describing to the
tribunes the advance on Rome of Coriolanus and his Volscian Army.

> *Com.*   He is their god. He leads them like a thing
>   Made by some other deity than Nature,
>   That shapes men better; and they follow him
>   Against us brats with no less confidence
>   Than boys pursuing summer butterflies,
>   Or butchers killing flies.

Thus it would seem evident that the childhood frustrations of
Coriolanus stand—and are seen by Shakespeare to stand—in a cause-
effect relationship to the unleashing of furious aggression in adult
life.

These hints as to the early history of the hero are again in marked
agreement with sequences frequently noted in the past history of the
phallic-narcissist. Reich remarks: "The infantile history regularly reveals serious disappointments in the object of the other sex, disappointments which occurred precisely at the time when attempts were
made to win the object through phallic exhibition. In men, one often
finds that the mother was the stronger of the parents, or the father
had died early or was otherwise out of the picture."

Before proceeding to a consideration of the interaction between the personality of Coriolanus and the events of the drama, it seems advisable to direct special attention to the character of Virgilia, since her role, although extremely brief in number of lines, is of great significance to the action of the play.

The personality contrast between Virgilia and Volumnia is revealed quite early in the drama (Act I, Scene III). When Volumnia has given the long speech quoted above about sending her son into battle at the age of sixteen, Virgilia breaks in with, "But had he died in the business, madam; how then?" And indeed one gathers from Volumnia's opening line ("I pray you, daughter, sing; or express yourself in a more comfortable sort"), that Virgilia's affectionate concern for her husband's well-being prevents her from taking the unfeminine delight in his military exploits which her mother-in-law shows to excess.

In addition to its presentation of the butterfly anecdote the scene appears expressly designed to show the contrast between Virgilia and Volumnia. The women's reaction to this very story of Valeria's is illuminating. Volumnia takes unadulterated pleasure in thinking that little Marcius is developing his father's fierceness, saying, "One on's father's moods." Virgilia's pleasure at Valeria's remarks appears to be mingled with misgivings, for her comment is "A crack, madam." When Valeria invites her to go out seeking amusement, Virgilia declines, plainly out of anxiety about her husband's dangerous situation. Volumnia is all for putting on a brave front, and she insists that her daughter-in-law go, but Virgilia shows herself capable of standing up to the older woman and courteously persists in her refusal.

The contrast is again pointed out in Act II, Scene I. Just before Coriolanus's return from his victory over the Volscians, Volumnia and Virgilia are conversing with Menenius.

> *Vol.* Look, here's a letter from him; the state hath another, his wife, another, and, I think, there's one at home for you.
>
> *Men.* I will make my very house reel tonight. A letter for me!
>
> *Vir.* Yes, certain, there's a letter for you; I saw 't.
>
> *Men.* A letter for me! . . . Is he not wounded? He was wont to come home wounded.
>
> *Vir.* O, no, no, no.
>
> *Vol.* O, he is wounded; I thank the gods for 't.

In addition to the obvious contrast between the reaction of Virgilia and that of Volumnia to the idea of Coriolanus's having been wounded, this scene indicates that Virgilia elicits a different response from Coriolanus than does his mother, i.e., the hero has not referred to his wounds in the letter to his wife.

A few moments later, when Coriolanus has appeared, Volumnia

becomes almost boisterous in her enjoyment of her son's honors and then quickly alludes to the one remaining one which she expects him to receive, the consulship. Virgilia, it may be inferred, shows quietly a much greater depth of feeling, but one altogether focussed on her husband and not on his honors. Coriolanus responds to her with the speech of which the first line has previously been quoted.

> *Cor.* My gracious silence, hail!
> Wouldst thou have laughed had I come coffin'd home,
> That weep'st to see me triumph? Ah, my dear,
> Such eyes the widows in Corioli wear,
> And mothers that lack sons.

A final point to be made in this connection is that whereas Volumnia figures prominently in urging Coriolanus to seek the consulship and to speak hypocritically to the tribunes and plebians in so doing, Virgilia takes no part in these maneuvers. In other words, in addition to having a greater capacity for tender affection than has Volumnia, Virgilia also exceeds her mother-in-law in certain qualities of dignity and integrity.

Thus, in summary, Virgilia appears much more feminine than does the mother of Coriolanus, less selfish in her relationship to her husband, more loving toward him, and less concerned with honors and appearances.

In a consideration of the relationship in which the action of the play stands to the personality of Coriolanus, it is convenient to divide the play into three sections: Acts I and II, Act III, and Acts IV and V. To keep within the limitations of a single paper, it will be necessary to concentrate on features of particular significance.

One such feature, which is fully developed in the early portions of the play, is the attitude of Coriolanus toward the plebians, partly expressed in the lines previously quoted as an example of his arrogance. There is marked tension and dislike mutual between Coriolanus and his patrician friends and the plebians and their tribunes, so much so that the play has sometimes been considered to be essentially a political one, with Coriolanus portraying a "typical tory who prefers the privileges of his class to the good of his country." Goddard points out that this view is superficially plausible, but will not stand up under close scrutiny. On the one hand, the interest in the drama is attached much more to character than to class. On the other, Coriolanus disqualifies himself as a typical tory with the following speech.

> *Cor.* Custom calls me to 't.
> What custom wills, in all things should we do 't,
> The dust on antique time would lie unswept

> And mountainous error be too highly heapt
> For truth to o'er-peer.

What then is the nature of Coriolanus's antipathy to the Roman plebians, and, specifically, to the plebians as a mob? One of his most specific statements on this point is that he sees the mob as "foes to nobleness." Since he is dedicated to a kind of nobility, this statement sounds as if the mob represents to him the personification of unacceptable impulses in his own personality. This idea is difficult to prove, but it receives some confirmation in another speech of Coriolanus.

> *Cor.* For this mutable, rank-scented many, let them
> Regard me as I do not flatter and
> Therein behold themselves.

A paraphrase of the latter part of this sentence, taken just at face value, would probably be: ". . . let them give heed to me, and, since I shall tell them the truth (about themselves) without flattery, they can see what they are really like." Yet when a *double entendre* such as this exists in a speech of one of Shakespeare's characters, it is often felt by critics that the character was conceived by the author as intending both meanings. It is my impression that such is the case here. Very likely Coriolanus is not to be thought of as aware of the second, the latent meaning of the speech, but he is nevertheless betraying his identification of the mob with repressed tendencies in himself.

If this idea appears plausible, it might be of value to consider some of the accusations Coriolanus levels at the plebians and to see if they would fit in logically as ego-alien (unconscious) tendencies in his own personality. The principal charges are that the plebians are cowardly, covetous, parasitic, and pleasure-loving: in other words, the diametric opposites of the surface features of Coriolanus's personality. This striking contrast does not in itself prove anything, but it is compatible with what has elsewhere been demonstrated to be true of phallic-narcissists in general, namely, that their overt behavior has an important defensive value against the opposite characteristics. Here again it is of interest to note a portion of Reich's original formulation.

> The phallic character does not regress. He remains at the phallic stage; more than that, he exaggerates his manifestations in order to protect himself against a regression to passivity and anality.

The last-named characteristics are clearly expressed in lay terms by Coriolanus's indictment of the plebians.

Another aspect of Coriolanus's estimate of the mob is that he considers it to be untrustworthy and childish. It is worthwhile to note that the two terms to which Coriolanus reacts with the greatest violence when applied to himself are "traitor" (Act III) and "boy" (Act V). The passages in question will be considered later, but it should be mentioned at this point that one receives a strong impression that Coriolanus is reacting on the basis of a major inner conflict at these times, inasmuch as the appelations are logically meaningless as regards his overt behavior.

A second point, closely related to the one concerning his attitude toward the mob and of crucial importance to the action of the drama, is the extreme aversion felt by Coriolanus to the prescribed behavior of begging for votes to obtain the consulship. Of this procedure the single feature most repulsive to the hero is the traditional showing to the crowd the wounds received in his country's service. Coriolanus's response to Volumnia when she first expresses the hope that he will receive the consulship reveals the close linkage between the two points.

> *Cor.*   Know, good mother,
> I had rather be their servant in my way
> Than sway with them in theirs.

During the scenes in which Coriolanus is urged to seek the office of consul and then does stand in the forum soliciting votes, it becomes rather clear that the aspect of the situation which he finds most intolerable is the being placed in the passive position. The defense-system by which his self-esteem is maintained cannot function under these conditions, whereas in the battle situation, in which the wounds were actually received, it functioned effectively.

The structural turning-point of the play occurs classically in Act III, Scene III. The preparation for the crisis has taken place during the final scene of the previous act and the first two scenes of Act III. Although the citizens had responded to Coriolanus's solicitation by giving him their votes initially, they quickly withdrew them under the skillful suasion of the envious and fearful tribunes. An altercation ensued between the plebians and tribunes on the one hand and Coriolanus and some patrician friends on the other, as a result of which Coriolanus was to stand trial as an enemy of the people. One is given to understand that the outcome is still very much in doubt, that reconciliation and even the consulship are still within reach for Coriolanus if he were to behave in a humble fashion at the trial. In response to his mother's plea, Coriolanus has reluctantly given his word to dissemble his pride, and at first does so.

> *Sic.*   I do demand
> If you submit you to the people's voices,
> Allow their officers, and are content
> To suffer lawful censure for such faults
> As shall be proved upon you?
> *Cor.*   I am content.

Menenius then speaks movingly in Coriolanus's behalf, but immediately thereafter the situation explodes.

> *Sic.*   We charge you, that you have contrived to take
> From Rome all season'd office and to wind
> Yourself a power tyrannical;
> For which you are a traitor to the people.
> *Cor.*   How! traitor!
> *Men.*   Nay, temperately; your promise.
> *Cor.*   The fires i' th' lowest hell fold in the people!
> Call me their traitor! Thou injurious tribune!
> Within thine eyes sat twenty thousand deaths,
> In thy hands clutched as many millions, in
> Thy lying tongue both numbers, I would say
> "Thou liest" unto thee with a voice as free
> As I do praise the gods.
> *Sic.*   Mark you this, people?
> *Plebians.*   To th' rock, to th' rock with him!

As mentioned above, the charges, taken literally, are rather wide of the mark. Coriolanus is not at all a contriver, and is not particularly interested in political power, *per se*. His violent reaction to the indictment is therefore the more remarkable and can only be understood as coming from powerful forces of the unconscious. The two key stimulus words for his outbreak are "Rome" and "traitor." To comprehend the hero's reaction, it appears of value to hypothesize an unconscious identification on his part of Rome with his mother, with the appellation, "traitor," then referring to an offense with regard to the mother, not Rome or its citizens. Such an identification is a fairly common one, and, in this instance, would be rendered especially likely by the patriotic posing of Volumnia, plus her emphasis on the martial virtues which were so highly regarded by the city-state.

If there does exist such an unconscious equation, the action of the drama is rendered more comprehensible. Coriolanus's entire life until Act II has involved an effort to prove that he wanted nothing from mother-Rome except to serve and defend her. During Acts II and III, and particularly in the crucial third scene of the latter, he is in the position of asking something from her. What he is asking is her full acceptance of him as consul, i.e., as father-figure. Moreover the immediate circumstances of his asking have strongly passive aspects. Thus, when the tribune accuses Coriolanus of being a traitor to Rome, the defense-system by which the hero has maintained his equilibrium is dealt a severe blow. The unconscious significance of the accusation appears to be that Coriolanus's acts have been entirely selfish and that what he has really wanted is exclusive possession of the mother. The charge strikes home the more readily for its coming at a time when Coriolanus has just set partially aside his arrogant pride, a quality which constituted his main line of defense against both passive yearnings and oedipal desires.

When Coriolanus leaves Rome at the end of Act III, he does so on a subdued note, a note of pathos, yet not without dignity. The idea of his avenging return to the city in force has not yet appeared. Act IV is chiefly concerned with the development and implementation of this idea. Several subordinate considerations are also developed; the change of heart of the plebians, who now feel that they were betrayed by the tribunes into banishing their natural leader; a further contrasting of the personalities of Volumnia and Virgilia; and the growth of an envious fear of Coriolanus on the part of Aufidius, who initially furnished the Roman with the means of revenge by placing him at the head of a Volscian army.[4] All in all, Act IV is a relatively quiet period between two emotional crises.

The intensely dramatic Act V is chiefly concerned with the successive pleas made to Coriolanus to abandon his revenge by those persons who mean the most to him: Cominius, Menenius, Virgilia, Volumnia, and little Marcius.

According to the hypothesis previously developed, the sack of Rome with the destruction of many of its inhabitants and the looting of its property would have the unconscious significance of (a regression to) sadism directed against the mother. The general impression of literary critics, that it is the long and impassioned speech of Volumnia in Scene III, a scene in which she goes down on her knees to her son, which changes Coriolanus's intention, is consonant with this hypothesis. The mother's abandoning her masculine behavior and asking her son's forgiveness and mercy could dissolve some of his unconscious hostility toward her as well as some of the conscious hostility toward Rome.

There are, however, subtler aspects involved in this change of

---

[4] There is some material suggestive of the hypothesis that Aufidius is unconsciously a father-substitute for Coriolanus, to whom the hero turns after the rejection by mother-Rome.

heart, to which, to the best of my knowledge, Goddard has been the
first to call attention. The first of these aspects is that Coriolanus is
not far from relenting even when visited by old Menenius, despite
his boast to Aufidius that his resolve will be proved to be unwaver-
ing. That such is the case is suggested by his attempt to communicate
with Menenius only in writing in order to avoid the interview and
also by his comment to Aufidius when Menenius departs.

> *Cor.*   This last old man,
> Whom with a crack'd heart I have sent to Rome,
> Lov'd me above the measure of a father.

Goddard remarks: "The ambiguity as to whose heart it was that was
cracked is plainly intentional on the poet's part, whatever it was on
Coriolanus'."

More importantly, Goddard presents evidence to suggest that the
roles of Virgilia and little Marcius are of considerable (perhaps of
decisive) importance in the crucial scene. The first point this critic
mentions in this connection is the purely technical one that Shakespeare "is not in the habit of giving the deciding voice to the utterer
of the longest speech—and Volumnia speaks about a hundred lines
in this scene." The second is based on the following exchange:

> *Vir.*   My lord and husband!
> *Cor.* These eyes are not the same I wore in Rome.
> *Vir.* The sorrow that delivers us thus changed
> Makes you think so.
> *Cor.*   Like a dull actor now
> I have forgot my part, and I am out,
> Even to a full disgrace.

In other words, Coriolanus indicates that he is on the verge of relenting before Volumnia makes her plea and in direct response to
his wife's presence. The rest of the speech is no less meaningful.

> *(Cor.)* .... Best of my flesh,
> Forgive my tyranny; but do not say
> For that, "Forgive our Roman." O, a kiss,
> Long as my exile, sweet as my revenge!
> Now, by the jealous queen of heaven, that kiss
> I carried from thee, dear; and my true lip
> Hath virgin'd it e'er since. You gods! I prate,
> And the most noble mother of the world
> Leave unsaluted. Sink, my knee, i' th' earth;
>   *(Kneels.)*

> Of thy deep duty more impression show
> Than that of common sons.

In Shakespeare's play Volumnia is left ungreeted until the embrace of Virgilia is over, whereas Plutarch's version states: "First he kissed his mother."

An additional point of interest in the above lines is contained in the words, "sweet as my revenge." If Virgilia's kiss means as much to Coriolanus as his contemplated revenge, perhaps the latter will be unnecessary.

Returning to Goddard's comments, one finds two additional points among the several he offers which warrant especial consideration. One of these is based on Coriolanus's interruption of Volumnia's lengthy plea.

> *Cor.* Not of a woman's tenderness to be,
> Requires nor child nor woman's face to see.
> I have sat too long. (*He rises.*)

Goddard notes that "tenderness" is "the last (word) in the language to fit Volumnia," and also "that it is of the effect of seeing a woman's face, not of hearing her voice, that he speaks shows again what force is converting him, for Virgilia, it will be remembered, he has named 'my gracious silence.' "

The other point is based on the final lines of Volumnia's speech, the ones just preceding Coriolanus's renunciation of his revenge.

> *(Vol.)* .... Come, let us go:
> This fellow had a Volscian to his mother;
> His wife is in Corioli, and his child
> Like him by chance.

The critic's comment is as follows:

> Why does Shakespeare seize just this moment to remind us of the likeness between father and child? Why but to show us what force has finally melted Coriolanus? A second more and he has capitulated. . . . Volumnia admits that the child is like the father. What she does not perceive is that the father is still like the child. Another mother and another son are acting through their very inaction over the heads of the apparent actors; the effective forces are the dove-like eyes of Virgilia. Her tears, her silence, the innocence of the boy and the innocent memories he stirs of another boy not yet utterly crushed by a false education and example. It is not the mother, then, who performs the miracle, nor the child. It is the mother-and-the-child.

The probability appears to be that Shakespeare intended us to regard Coriolanus's change of intent as the result of two forces, one deriving from the unaccustomed position of the hero's mother and the other from the long-term effects of the relationship with Virgilia. To put these concepts in psychological terminology, one might say that through his marriage to the emotionally healthy and feminine Virgilia, Coriolanus has had a "corrective emotional experience" and has undergone a partial emotional maturation with a lessening of the need for exhibitionistic, pseudo-masculine behavior, a partial alteration in his concept of woman (mother), and an increase in his capacity for object-love. Under the peculiarly great stresses comprising the greater part of the play, the old, morbid influences deriving from Volumnia produce pathological responses in abundance. Yet the healthier influences of the marriage have not been without effect and make possible the relenting which takes place in the final act.

Because of the complexity of ideas here involved, perhaps an attempt at restatement is permissible. Coriolanus's plan to take Rome by force and destroy it is rendered less necessary once he has brought his mother to her knees, according to the previously suggested equation of Rome with mother. Nevertheless, if it had not been for the maturing effect of the relationship with Virgilia, the hostility of Coriolanus would probably have been sufficiently great to have demanded both forms of revenge.

The foregoing speculations are again reminiscent of what Reich has to say regarding therapeutic modification of the phallic-narcissist.

> The analytic treatment of phallic-narcissistic characters is one of the most thankful tasks. Since the phallic phase has been fully reached and since aggression is relatively free, the establishment of genital and social potency, other things being equal, is easier than in other forms. The analysis is always successful if one succeeds in unmasking the phallic-narcissistic attitudes as a defense against passive-feminine tendencies and in eliminating the unconscious tendency of revenge against the other sex.

It appears likely from the evidence the play affords that Virgilia has, to a slight but significant extent, increased Coriolanus's awareness of softer tendencies in himself and has reduced his need for revenge against women.

It remains to be asked, what role does guilt play in determining Coriolanus's behavior in the final act of the play? The evidence on this score is somewhat inconclusive, although there can be no question but that such feelings are of significance. Coriolanus's speech of capitulation is the most revealing in this connection.

> (*He holds her by the hand, silent.*)

Cor.   O mother, mother!
> What have you done? Behold the heavens do ope,
> The gods look down, and this unnatural scene
> They laugh at. O my mother, mother! O!
> You have won a happy victory for Rome;
> But, for your son,—believe it, O, believe it,
> Most dangerously you have with him prevailed,
> If not most mortal to him. But, let it come.
> Aufidius, though I cannot make true wars,
> I'll frame convenient peace. Now, good Aufidius,
> Were you in my stead, would you have heard
> A mother less, or granted less, Aufidius?

Auf.   I was mov'd withal.

Cor.   I dare be sworn you were;
> And, sir, it is no little thing to make
> Mine eyes to sweat compassion. But, good sir,
> What peace you'll make, advise me. For my part,
> I'll not to Rome, I'll back with you; and pray you,
> Stand to me in this cause. O mother! wife!

> (*Speaks apart with them.*)

The appellation, "unnatural scene," suggests guilt. More importantly, so does the determination to return to Corioli, inasmuch as this decision has in it an element of possible suicide. If the implications of this final move were entirely clear, one could make a more definite statement quantitatively about the importance of the guilt feelings. The implications are not entirely clear, however. Coriolanus consults with Aufidius about the terms of peace. He is actually welcomed by the Volscian populace on his return to Corioli, and apparently would have come off unscathed but for the treachery of Aufidius. Moreover, the general reaction of both critics and audiences to the final portion of the play, particularly to Act V, Scene III, is, as previously noted in the quotation from Bradley, one of "reconciliation . . . and exaltation." All that one can say with assurance, therefore, is that guilt feelings are important but probably not decisive in the final crisis.

There remains to be considered the last scene of the play, in which Coriolanus is taunted by Aufidius and then murdered by the conspirators. The portion of particular interest is the passage between Aufidius and Coriolanus just before the murder.

Auf.   . . . . tell the traitor, in the highest degree
> He hath abused your powers.

Cor.	"Traitor!" How now!
Auf.	Ay, traitor, Marcius!
Cor.	Marcius!
Auf.	Ay, Marcius, Caius Marcius! Dost thou think

       I'll grace thee with that robbery, thy stolen name,
       Coriolanus, here in Corioli?
       You lords and heads o' the state, perfidiously
       He has betrayed your business, and given up,
       For certain drops of salt, your city Rome,
       I say "your city," to his wife and mother.
       ....At his nurse's tears
       He whin'd and roared away your victory....

Cor.	Hear'st thou, Mars?
Auf.	Name not the god, thou boy of tears!
Cor.	Ha!
Auf.	No more.
Cor.	Measureless liar, thou hast made my heart

       Too great for what contains it. Boy! O slave!
       Pardon me, lords, 'tis the first time that ever
       I was forced to scold. Your judgements, my grave lords,
       Must give this cur the lie; and his own notion—
       Who wears my stripes impressed upon him, that
       Must bear my beating to his grave—shall join
       To thrust the lie upon him.

First Lord. Peace, both, and hear me speak.

Cor. Cut me to pieces, Volsces; men and lads,
       Stain all your edges on me. Boy! False hound!
       If you have writ your annals true, 'tis there
       That, like an eagle in a dove-cote, I
       Fluttered your Volsces in Corioli;
       Alone I did it. Boy!

It appears worthy of note that, although Shakespeare strives for realism and dramatic effect above lyricism throughout most of the play, at this moment all three qualities are combined superbly to produce a passage which is scarcely excelled elsewhere in his writings and contains a metaphor which has "passed into the common speech of man."

What are the words which stimulate Coriolanus to this eloquent fury? There is the previously effective "traitor," but there is the still more effective "boy." Coriolanus speaks the latter word three times in his outburst, and it is linked with the reference to his mother as "nurse." Doubtless Coriolanus is not aware of the reason for the peculiar effectiveness of this appellation in releasing such a torrent of feeling, but Shakespeare surely is. Taking into consideration the dignity and nobility which find expression in the speech along with the rage and traces of the old pseudo-masculinity, one can only feel that it is the supremely bitter irony of the situation which stirs Coriolanus: that he should be accused of being a boy in connection with his nearest approach to emotional maturity.[5] . . .

[5] Since the Elizabethans and Jacobeans divided the members of society into two categories, men, and women-and-boys,—with much emphasis on virile and effeminate qualities,—when a Shakespearean character uses the term, "boy," in such an instance as this, it carries the additional implication of "effeminate." There is thus the further irony that Coriolanus should be accused of effeminacy in connection with his nearest approach to a compassionate masculinity.

PART TWO

View Points

THEME AND STRUCTURE

Kenneth Burke: Coriolanus—and the Delights of Faction

In conclusion, then, where are we? We have been considering Coriolanus' qualifications as a scapegoat, whose symbolic sacrifice is designed to afford an audience pleasure. We have suggested: (1) His primary role as a cathartic vessel resides in the excessiveness with which he forces us to confront the discriminatory motives intrinsic to society as we know it. (2) There is a sheerly "expressive" kind of catharsis in his way of giving form to the complexities of *family, class,* and *national* motives as they come to a focus in the self-conflicts of an *individual*. (3) There is the "curative" function of invective as such, when thus released under controlled conditions that transform the repressed into the expressed, yet do us no damage. And (4) the attempt has been made to consider the "paradox of substance" whereby the chosen scapegoat can "be himself" and arrive at the end "proper to his nature" only if many events and other persons "conspire" to this end, the persons by being exactly the kind of persons they are, and the events by developing in the exact order in which they do develop. To sum it all up, then, in a final formula for tragic catharsis: (a formula that I wrote with such a play as *Coriolanus* in mind, though it could be applied *mutatis mutandis* to other texts):[1]

Take some pervasive unresolved tension typical of a given social order (or of life in general). While maintaining the "thought" of it in its over-all importance, reduce it to terms of personal conflict (conflict between friends, or members of the same family). Feature some prominent figure who, in keeping with his character, though possessing admirable qualities, carries this conflict to excess. Put him in a situation that points

---

"*Coriolanus—and the Delights of Faction.*" From Language as Symbolic Action by *Kenneth Burke (Berkeley: University of California Press, 1968), p. 94. Reprinted by permission of The Regents of the University of California.*

[1] Originally printed in *Arts in Society,* Vol. 2, No. 3 (Univ. of Wisconsin Press, 1963).

up the conflict. Surround him with a cluster of characters whose relations
to him and to one another help motivate and accentuate his excesses.
So arrange the plot that, after a logically motivated turn, his excesses
lead necessarily to his downfall. Finally, suggest that his misfortune will
be followed by a promise of general peace.

CAIUS MARCIUS CORIOLANUS

T. S. Eliot: Coriolan II: Difficulties of a Statesman

Cry what shall I cry?
All flesh is grass: comprehending
The Companions of the Bath, the Knights of the British Empire,
    the Cavaliers,
O Cavaliers! of the Legion of Honour,
The Order of the Black Eagle (1st and 2nd class),
And the Order of the Rising Sun.
Cry cry what shall I cry?
The first thing to do is to form the committees:
The consultative councils, the standing committees, select committees
    and sub-committees.
One secretary will do for several committees.
What shall I cry?
Arthur Edward Cyril Parker is appointed telephone operator
At a salary of one pound ten a week rising by annual increments
    of five shillings
To two pounds ten a week; with a bonus of thirty shillings at Christ-
    mas
And one week's leave a year.
A committee has been appointed to nominate a commission of en-
    gineers
To consider the Water Supply.
A commission is appointed
For Public Works, chiefly the question of rebuilding the fortifica-
    tions.

A commission is appointed
To confer with a Volscian commission
About perpetual peace: the fletchers and javelin-makers and smiths
Have appointed a joint committee to protest against the reduction
    of orders.
Meanwhile the guards shake dice on the marches
And the frogs (O Mantuan) croak in the marshes.
Fireflies flare against the faint sheet lightning
What shall I cry?
Mother mother
Here is the row of family portraits, dingy busts, all looking remark-
    ably Roman,
Remarkably like each other, lit up successively by the flare
Of a sweaty torchbearer, yawning.
O hidden under the . . . Hidden under the . . .
    Where the dove's foot rested and locked for a moment,
A still moment, repose of noon, set under the upper branches of
    noon's widest tree
Under the breast feather stirred by the small wind after noon
There the cyclamen spreads its wings, there the clematis droops over
    the lintel
O mother (not among these busts, all correctly inscribed)
I a tired head among these heads
Necks strong to bear them
Noses strong to break the wind
Mother
May we not be some time, almost now, together,
If the mactations, immolations, oblations, impetrations,
Are now observed
May we not be
O hidden
Hidden in the stillness of noon, in the silent croaking night.
Come with the sweep of the little bat's wing, with the small flare of
    the firefly or lightning bug,
"Rising and falling, crowned with dust," the small creatures,
The small creatures chirp thinly through the dust, through the night.

O mother
What shall I cry?
We demand a committee, a representative committee, a committee of
    investigation

             RESIGN   RESIGN   RESIGN

Paul A. Jorgensen: Shakespeare's Coriolanus: Elizabethan Soldier

We are of course made to feel the splendid strength of Coriolanus in battle, but eulogies of his generalship are consistently limited. His fellow commander, Titus Lartius, admires his "grim looks" and the "thunder-like percussion" of his sounds (I, iv, 58–59).[1] The enemy leader, Titus Aufidius, observes that his antagonist "fights dragon-like" (IV, vii, 22). And Volumnia, a careful student of her son's wars, envisions him plucking Aufidius "down by th' hair," stamping, and calling "Come on, you cowards!" (I, iii, 33–36). These accounts suggest a lone, ardent fighter. Concerning wise leadership, the eulogies are silent. The limited nature of Coriolanus' military genius is dramatically evident in the battle scenes. His simple, ardent pugnacity is indicated when Aufidius' offensive makes him "sweat with wrath" (I, iv, 27). When the Romans are beaten back to their trenches, "Enter *Marcius,* cursing." And his most famous exploit, entering the gates of Corioles without support, befits an adventurer rather than a general. Plutarch's Coriolanus, in fact, does not enter the city alone. And it is not unlikely that in thus enhancing the daring of his hero, Shakespeare was recognizing and exploiting Coriolanus' resemblance to Elizabethan military adventurers.

Some such parallels were too close to have escaped any contemporary audience. Essex, a brilliant fighter and bad general, habitually led rather than directed the charge.[2] The audience might also have recalled Grenville's daring command of the *Revenge.* According to the Dutch Jan van Linschoten, who saw the battle, Grenville "went into the Spanish fleete, and shot among them, doing them great hurte, and thinking the rest would have followed: which they did not, but left him there and sayled away."[3] Grenville's fierce personality, moreover, would account not only for the desperateness of the attempt,

---

"Shakespeare's Coriolanus: Elizabethan Soldier" by Paul A. Jorgensen. From PMLA *64 (1949): 221–22. Reprinted by permission of the Modern Language Association of America.*

[1] I have used the *Complete Works,* ed. Kittredge (Boston, 1936).

[2] "My Lord of Essex was one of the first that got over the walls, followed by the souldiers as the place would give them leave"—*The Commentaries of Sir Francis Vere* (Cambridge, 1657), p. 39, Cf. p. 58.

[3] "The Fight and Cyclone at Azores," *Arber's English Reprints* (London, 1871), p. 90.

but for his unpopularity as a leader. According to the nonpartisan Linschoten,

> he was a man very unquiet in his minde, and greatly affected to warre: . . . he had performed many valiant actes, and was greatly feared in these Islands, and knowne of every man, but of nature very severe, so that his owne people hated him for his fierceness, and spake verie hardly of him.[4]

Another commander, Edward Stanley, entered a breach by catching the head of a Spaniard's pike, trying to wrench it from his foe's grasp amidst the constant entertainment of pike thrusts and bullets, and then allowing himself to be hoisted over the parapet where he held off the enemy until he was joined by his fellows.[5] Coriolanus' single-handed entry into Corioles would have seemed to Shakespeare's audience no mere tale of legendary heroism.

VOLUMNIA

Rufus Putney: Coriolanus and His Mother

Late in his career Shakespeare turned to the legend of the prehistoric Roman hero, Coriolanus, who, in deference to his mother's entreaties, abandoned his vengeance and spared ungrateful Rome. It is a tragedy ensuing from an œdipal mother-son relationship. Volumnia, the mother, is a consumingly fierce, domineering woman and mother. Widowed when her only son was an infant, she reared him to be a harsh, contemptuous, intolerant, arrogant patrician and a ferocious, indomitable warrior. Upon this mighty man she then imposed the role of submissive son who must obey his mother and strive for her constant approbation. She so imposed her values upon him that she created in him a superego that made him a man of iron rigidity. Since his conscience does not permit compromises, he is a military hero but a failure as politician and statesman. Volumnia ultimately contrives his doom.

When extreme conflict arises between them because she can sacri-

---

"Coriolanus and His Mother" by *Rufus Putney. From* The Psychoanalytic Quarterly *31 (1962): 380–81. Reprinted by permission of* The Psychoanalytic Quarterly.

[4] *Ibid.,* pp. 91–92. Like Coriolanus (as seen by the tribunes), Grenville was a "man of intolerable pride and insatiable ambition"—Lane to Walsyngham, Sept. 8, 1585, *Cal. State Papers (Col.),* 1, 3.

[5] J. W. Fortescue, *A History of the British Army* (London, 1910), I, 149–150.

fice her principles to the demands of reality while he, so thoroughly
has been the process of introjection, cannot, she makes the charge that
he is causing her death, or that she will commit suicide to force his
submission. So stringent is the conflict between his conscience and his
unconscious death wishes—Volumnia had sent him at sixteen to his
first battle and gloried in his wounds and scars—that he automatically
submits. On a second occasion, when at the head of the Volscian
army, he is at the gates of helpless Rome, which he has vowed to
destroy in revenge for his banishment, she renews her threats to overcome the stubbornness with which he clings to his desire for vengeance. Although her threat that she will commit suicide as soon as
he advances on Rome has more probability than her former com-
plaint that she would be killed if he caused civil war in Rome,
Coriolanus tries to resist because he knows now he must choose between his death and hers. Ultimately, his conscience compels him to
choose his own death rather than his mother's.

The hidden theme of matricide has not been noted in previous
discussions of the play, although other aspects of the œdipal situation
have been well presented, especially by Hofling.[1] Hitherto, the rigidity
and exorbitance of Coriolanus's conscience have not received due
emphasis; nor has his perfectionism, the need for absolute accomplishment imposed on him by his conscience, been offered as the explanation of his inability to tolerate hearing himself praised.

THE CITIZENS

'A. A. Smirnov: Shakespeare:
A Marxist Interpretation

Like Hamlet, Cordelia, and Othello, Coriolanus knows only one
law, the law of honour and truth, and in this he is at one with
Shakespeare. This does not mean, however, that Shakespeare agrees
with Coriolanus in his fierce hatred of the people and the betrayal
of his country which this implies thereby.

The whole play contradicts such a conception. To the unprejudiced
reader, the Roman plebeians are portrayed in the tragedy with rare

From Shakespeare: A Marxist Interpretation *by A. A. Smirnov, translated by
Sonia Volochova, The Critics' Group Series, no. 2 (1936), pp. 76–78.*

[1] Hofling, Charles K.: *An Interpretation of Shakespeare's* Coriolanus. *American
Imago*, XIV, 1957, pp. 407–35. [See this volume, pp. 84–99.]

sympathy, and, moreover, with a profound understanding of their socio-historical position. Of course, the plebeians are not yet politically mature, nor are they distinguished for military prowess, but, in their struggles with the patricians, Shakespeare's sympathies are all on their side.

As if to preclude any possible misunderstanding,—which nevertheless arose—in the very first lines of the play, which are as significant as the last, Shakespeare has the plebeians express their demands fully, in such a way that his own attitude towards them remains clear until the end. One of them exclaims (I, 1):

> One word, good citizens.

But another interrupts him:

> We are accounted poor citizens; the patricians good. What authority surfeits on would relieve us: if they would yield us but the superfluity, while it were wholesome, we might guess they relieved us humanely; but they think we are too dear: the leanness that afflicts us, the object of our misery, is an inventory to particularize their abundance; our sufferance is a gain to them.—Let us revenge this with our pikes ere we become rakes: for the gods know I speak this in hunger for bread, not in thirst for revenge.

One can find no hypocrisy in such words, and the poet who can write them must be in sympathy with them. . . .

Coriolanus persists in his blindness; if he finally gives in to his mother's supplications, he does so only because of compassion for her rather than because of patriotic impulse. The blind, anarchistic Coriolanus is motivated by personal, not social, considerations; Shakespeare therefore, condemns him unequivocally, despite his magnitude.

Coriolanus is one of Shakespeare's gloomiest tragedies. It reflects his profound disillusionment with absolutism, the court, the state officials, and the upper classes, as is evidenced by the total absence of positive characters drawn from the privileged classes. Collectively, the plebeians constitute the only positive force in the play. Their political immaturity, however, disturbs Shakespeare, because they are still extremely credulous, simple-minded and inconstant. Shakespeare expresses this (I, 1) at the appearance of Menenius Agrippa, the most dangerous enemy of the people; a citizen announces (I, 1):

> Worthy Menenius Agrippa, one that hath always loved the people.

And another hastens to corroborate him:

> He's one honest enough; would all the rest were so!

The people allow themselves to be dazzled by the exploits of Coriolanus and trustingly give him their votes.

There is, however, a tremendous difference between Shakespeare's depiction of the masses in *Henry IV*, Part 2 (1591), or even in *Julius Caesar* (1599), and *Coriolanus* (1607). In fifteen years Shakespeare's political ideology had advanced as much as had the class consciousness of the English masses.

Brents Stirling: The Populace in Shakespeare

. . . With due respect for the claims of those who see in this play a balance—a satire against arrogant aristocracy as well as against a bungling populace; with deference also to the judgment of interpreters who insist that its antipopular speeches are simply in character, *Coriolanus* is still a morose play, and the scurrility leveled at the citizens is felt to be coldly cynical when compared with the vivid horseplay of the Cade scenes, or even with *Julius Caesar*. *Coriolanus* is an historical as well as a dramatic phenomenon and, like the Cade scenes, it deserves to be set in a perspective of events and of public response to them. The unsettled character of this period is, of course, well known but it would be well if a more specific climate of opinion, that of concern over the populace, were established as background.

In 1605 the Venetian secretary in England reported, probably incorrectly, "that a great revolution is on the point of breaking out in this kingdom" and that "the strongest suspicion of responsibility for this falls on the Puritans." [1] Another Venetian envoy reported two years later of the Northampton rising that the revolt was in serious danger of spreading, "thanks to the diverse religions which exist in this kingdom where the Puritans are expanding continually." The running account concludes with an opinion that the rising "has been growing to such an extent that they only require a leader to make it a formidable and open rebellion." [2]

Coriolanus is contemporaneous with widely felt enclosure riots of which the Venetian representative, as quoted above, takes account. . . . That *Coriolanus*, a play in which the plebeians resolve in the

From The Populace in Shakespeare *by Brents Stirling (New York: Columbia University Press, 1949), pp. 125–26, 127–28. Copyright 1949 by Columbia University Press. Reprinted by permission of the publisher.*

[1] *C.S.P. Venetian,* 1603–1607, p. 219.

[2] *Ibid.,* 1607–1610, pp. 6, 8.

first scene "rather to die than to famish" and in which they later weaken Rome's defenses, should have appeared in such an atmosphere of concern could be more than a coincidence. The acuteness of the enclosure problem, the resultant hunger and deprivation, and the ensuing riots which produced responses such as those of the Venetian envoy and of Wilkinson—all these factors contribute to an attitude of receptivity for such a play. We may let two official declarations complete the picture. It is probably not accidental that about the time *Coriolanus* appeared, a royal proclamation declared, "It is a thing notorious that many of the meanest sort of our people . . . have presumed lately to assemble themselves riotously in multitudes." [3] This proclamation asserted further that "the glory and strength of all kings consisteth in the multitude of subjects." Nor may it be coincidental that less than a month later another royal proclamation asserted, much in the vein of *Coriolanus,* that "of all other seditions and rebellions none doth bring such infinite waste and desolation upon a kingdom or state as these popular insurrections, which though they do seldom shake or endanger a crown, yet they do bring a heap of calamities upon multitudes of innocent subjects, and chiefly upon the authors and actors themselves." [4]

Menenius

Derek Traversi: Coriolanus

Menenius' rebuke, in the first verse speech of the play, is a suitable prelude to his fable. It assumes that the position by which his own class stands to benefit belongs to the natural and unalterable order of things. If, unlike some of his fellow-patricians, Menenius can show himself benignly human in dealing with those whom he assumes to be his inferiors, he is none the less the spokesman of a class which accepts the perpetuity of that close rigid view of social relations from which it profits. His habitual kindliness should not blind us to the touch of iron which this first utterance conveys. He takes it for granted that it is the duty of himself and his like to exercise "charitable care" over the people; but his concept of "charity," kindly and condescend-

---

"Coriolanus." From Shakespeare: The Roman Plays *by Derek Traversi (London: Hollis and Carter, Ltd., 1963), pp. 211–12. Copyright 1963 by Derek Traversi. Reprinted by permission of The Bodley Head Ltd.*

[3] Proclamation of June 28, 1607.
[4] Proclamation of July 24, 1607.

ing so long as it is unquestioned, is compatible with the denial of
responsibility when "charity" is not enough:

> For your wants,
> Your suffering in this dearth, you may as well
> Strike at the heaven with your staves as lift them
> Against the Roman state; whose course will on
> The way it takes, cracking ten thousand curbs
> Of more strong link asunder than can ever
> Appear in your impediment. For the dearth,
> The gods, not the patricians make it, and
> Your knees to them, not arms, must help.   [I. i. 70]

The effect is more searching in its revelation of complacency than
may at once appear. Rhythm and expression combine to embody the
irresistible motion of an impersonal and overbearing force with which
the speaker finally feels himself identified. The effect of the division
in the earlier part of the speech between "cracking" and "asunder,"
both words which carry a strong sense of violent physical separation,
is to convey an impression of ruthless progress, leading us to partake
directly in the advance of the state towards a goal conceived of as
barely human, dedicated to an indifferent fatality. The emotional
impetus so generated is then brought to a sudden curb after "impedi-
ment": the long period comes to an emphatic pause in the middle of
its implacable development and Menenius, turned from the bland
counsellor into the mouthpiece of an unrelenting social destiny,
throws upon the "gods" the responsibility for a catastrophe which no
thought of human solidarity is allowed to mitigate.

THE TRIBUNES

John Palmer: Political Characters
of Shakespeare

For the tribunes only one course of action is politically possible.
The election is not yet confirmed. If they are not once and for all to
accept their defeat, they must advise the citizens to reconsider their
promises to vote for Marcius. There is no fault to be found with

"Political Characters of Shakespeare." From Political and Comic Characters of
Shakespeare *by John Palmer (London: Macmillan & Co., Ltd., 1945), pp. 273–74.
Reprinted by permission of Macmillan & Co., Ltd., The Macmillan Company of
Canada Limited, and St. Martin's Press, Inc.*

their conduct of the situation. It is good, sound electioneering and
it is a happy politician who has nothing worse upon his conscience. . . .

    Brutus.   You should have said
        That as his worthy deeds did claim no less
        Than what he stood for, so his gracious nature
        Would think upon you for your voices and
        Translate his malice towards you into love,
        Standing your friendly lord.
    Sicinius.   Thus to have said,
        As you were fore-advis'd, had touch'd his spirit
        And tried his inclination; from him pluck'd
        Either his gracious promise, which you might,
        As cause had call'd you up, have held him to;
        Or else it would have gall'd his surly nature,
        Which easily endures not article
        Tying him to aught; so, putting him to rage,
        You should have ta'en the advantage of his choler,
        And pass'd him unelected.
    Brutus. Get you hence instantly, and tell those friends
        They have chose a consul that will from them take
        Their liberties; make them of no more voice
        Than dogs that are as often beat for barking
        As therefore kept to do so.
    Sicinius.   Let them assemble;
        And, on a safer judgement, all revoke
        Your ignorant election: enforce his pride,
        And his old hate unto you; besides, forget not
        With what contempt he wore the humble weed,
        How in his suit he scorn'd you; but your loves,
        Thinking upon his services, took from you
        The apprehension of his present portance.

The tribunes, in urging the people to revoke the election, counsel
them to attribute their mistake to the advice of their leaders:

        Say, you chose him
    More after our commandment than as guided
    By your own true affections; and that your minds,
    Pre-occupied with rather what you must do
    Than what you should, made you against the grain
    To voice him consul: lay the fault on us.

This last piece of advice from the tribunes to the citizens has frequently been denounced. Some critics go so far as to interpret it as
a false and cowardly attempt by a brace of mean-spirited rogues to

stand well with both sides. Admittedly it is dishonest. But do political leaders in the heat of an election always tell the truth? There is assuredly no question of double-dealing. The tribunes merely wish to provide the citizens with a reasonable excuse for revoking their choice. They also want the senators to feel that the rejection of Marcius is a spontaneous and representative act of the people. Is this manœuvre so uncommonly disgraceful? They are men in a desperate situation and they are honestly convinced that, if they allow the election to be confirmed, the inevitable popular reaction against Marcius will be all the more disastrous when it comes. Their motives—and they are good motives as far as they go—are plainly stated:

> *Brutus.* This mutiny were better put in hazard
> Than stay, past doubt, for greater:
> If, as his nature is, he fall in rage
> With their refusal, both observe and answer
> The vantage of his anger.
>
> *Sicinius.* To the Capitol, come:
> We will be there before the stream o' the people;
> And this shall seem, as partly 'tis, their own,
> Which we have goaded onward.

These, then, are the tactics of the popular front.

VIRGILIA

John Middleton Murry: Coriolanus

Of all the characters in *Coriolanus* one alone can be said to be truly congenial; and she is the least substantial of them all. Virgilia, Coriolanus's wife, though she is present throughout the whole of four scenes, speaks barely a hundred words. But a sudden, direct light is cast upon her by a lovely phrase when Coriolanus welcomes her on his triumphant return from Corioli as "My gracious silence!" Magical words! They give substance to our fleeting, fading glimpses of a vision which seems to tremble away from the clash of arms and pride that reverberates through the play. Behind the haughty warrior and his Amazonian mother, behind the vehement speech of this double Lucifer, the exquisite, timid spirit of Virgilia shrinks out of sight

"Coriolanus." *From* John Clare and Other Studies *by John Middleton Murry (London: Peter Nevill Limited, 1950), pp. 232–34. Reprinted by permission of The Society of Authors as the literary representative of the Estate of John Middleton Murry.*

into the haven of her quiet home. One can almost hear the faint
click of the door behind her as it shuts her from the noise of brawling
tongues. Yet at moments in her presence, and in the memory of her
presence, Coriolanus becomes another and a different being. It is true
we may listen in vain for other words so tender as "My gracious
silence!" from his lips. But in the heat of victorious battle, when
Coriolanus would clasp Cominius in his arms for joy, he discovers
in himself another splendid phrase to remember his happiness with
Virgilia.

> Oh! let me clip ye
> In arms as sound as when I woo'd, in heart
> As merry, as when our nuptial day was done
> And tapers burned to bedward.

And even in the anguish of the final struggle between his honour and
his heart, when his wife comes with his mother to intercede for Rome,
it is in the very accents of passionate devotion that he cries to Virgilia,

> Best of my flesh!
> Forgive my tyranny; but do not say,
> "For that forgive our Romans," Oh! a kiss
> Long as my exile, sweet as my revenge!
> Now, by the jealous queen of heaven, that kiss
> I carried from thee, dear, and my true lip
> Hath virgin'd it e'er since.

In the proud, unrelenting man of arms these sudden softenings are
wonderful. They conjure up the picture of a more reticent and self-
suppressed Othello, and we feel that, to strike to the heart through
Coriolanus's coat of mail, it needed an unfamiliar beauty of soul, a
woman whose delicate nature stood apart, untouched by the broils
and furies of her lord's incessant battling with the Roman people
and the enemies of Rome.

AUFIDIUS

Eugene M. Waith: The Herculean Hero

The change in emphasis from history to the heroic is clearly evident
in Shakespeare's treatment of Aufidius. In Plutarch's account he is not

From The Herculean Hero *by Eugene M. Waith (New York: Columbia University Press; London: Chatto & Windus, Ltd., 1962), pp. 130–32. Copyright ©
1962 by Eugene Waith. Reprinted by permission of the publishers.*

mentioned until the time of the banishment, when Coriolanus offers himself as a general to the Volsces. At this point, however, Plutarch states that Aufidius was noble and valiant, that the two had often encountered in battle and that they had "a marvellous private hate one against the other." [1] From these hints Shakespeare makes the figure of the worthy antagonist, who is a part of the story of so many heroes. The rivalry is mentioned in the very first scene of the play, and is made one of the deepest motives of the hero's conduct. He envies the nobility of Aufidius,

> And were I anything but what I am,
> I would wish me only he. . . .
> Were half to half the world by th'ears, and he
> Upon my party, I'd revolt, to make
> Only my wars with him. He is a lion
> That I am proud to hunt.   (I, 1, 235–40)

To fight with Aufidius is the ultimate test of Coriolanus' valour—of his warrior's areté. And because the rival warrior most nearly shares his own ideals, the relationship takes on an intense intimacy. Shakespeare introduces Aufidius unhistorically into the battle at Corioles. We discover that although Aufidius reciprocates the feelings of Coriolanus, he is prepared after his defeat at Corioles to use dishonourable means, if necessary, to destroy his enemy, but of this Coriolanus knows nothing, nor is there any hint of it when Aufidius later welcomes Coriolanus as an ally:

> Let me twine
> Mine arms about that body whereagainst
> My grained ash an hundred times hath broke
> And scarr'd the moon with splinters. . . .
>
>   .   .   .   ,   .
>
> Know thou first,
> I lov'd the maid I married; never man
> Sigh'd truer breath. But that I see thee here,
> Thou noble thing, more dances my rapt heart
> Than when I first my wedded mistress saw
> Bestride my threshold.   (IV, 5, 111–14, 118–23)

Plutarch's Aufidius makes only a brief and formal speech acknowledging the honour Coriolanus does him. Shakespeare's invention of a long speech, loaded with the metaphors of love, is the more striking at this point, since the preceding speech by Coriolanus follows Plutarch

[1] *Shakespeare's Plutarch,* ed. C. F. Tucker Brooke (New York, Duffield, 1909), II, 176.

very closely indeed. The strong bond between the rival warriors is obviously important.

It is sometimes thought highly ironic that Coriolanus, who prides himself on his constancy, should be guilty of the supreme inconstancy of treason to his country. In fact, however reprehensible he may be, he is not inconstant. Shakespeare makes it clear that his first allegiance is always to his personal honour. The fickleness of the mob and the scheming of the tribunes have deprived him of his deserts, much as Agamemnon's seizure of Briseis deprives Achilles. Both this threat to his honour and an ambivalent love-hatred draw Coriolanus to the enemy whom he considers almost an alter ego.

Resemblances or fancied resemblances between the two warriors establish the supremacy of the heroic ideal in Coriolanus' scale of values, but we cannot doubt which of them more nearly encompasses the ideal. As we watch the progress of their alliance, we see Aufidius becoming increasingly jealous and finally working for the destruction of his rival even while he treats him almost as a mistress. In defence of his conduct he asserts that Coriolanus has seduced his friends with flattery, but there is no evidence to support this unlikely accusation. Malice and double-dealing are quite absent from the nature of Coriolanus.

Chronology of Important Dates

	Shakespeare	The Age
1564	April 26: christened at Stratford.	Christopher Marlowe born.
1576		First public playhouse, The Theatre, built by James Burbage.
1579		Sir Thomas North's translation of Plutarch's *Lives*.
1582	Married to Anne Hathaway.	
1583	May 26: daughter Susanna christened.	
1585	February 2: twins, Hamnet and Judith, christened.	
1588		Defeat of the Spanish Armada.
1590		Edmund Spenser, *The Faerie Queene*, Books I–III.
1592	First reference to Shakespeare as an actor and playwright in London, by Robert Greene.	
1593	*Venus and Adonis* published.	Death of Christopher Marlowe.
1594	Membership in the Lord Chamberlain's company of actors. *Titus Andronicus* published.	Henry IV (of Navarre) crowned King of France.
1596	Obtained a grant of arms for his father.	
1597		First edition of Bacon's *Essays*.

1598	Praised by Francis Meres as leading English playwright.	
1599	Globe Theater built, with Shakespeare as a principal shareholder. *Julius Caesar* first performed.	Death of Edmund Spenser.
1601	Death of father, John Shakespeare.	Rebellion and death of the Earl of Essex.
1603	Lord Chamberlain's Men become the King's Men. *Hamlet* first published.	Death of Elizabeth I, and accession of James I.
1605		November 5: Guy Fawkes' "Gunpowder Plot" to blow up Parliament.
1607–8	*Antony and Cleopatra* first performed.	
1608	Death of mother, Mary Arden.	
1608–9	*Coriolanus* first performed.	
1611	Last complete play, *The Tempest*, first performed.	The Authorized (King James) Version of the Bible published.
1616	April 23: death of Shakespeare in Stratford.	
1623	First Folio edition of plays published.	

Notes on the Editor and Contributors

JAMES E. PHILLIPS, editor of this volume, is Professor of English at the University of California, Los Angeles, and author of books and articles on Shakespeare, Mary Queen of Scots, Spenser, Sidney, and Elizabethan drama.

KENNETH BURKE is a poet, critic, and lecturer whose influential theoretical studies include *Philosophy of Literary Form* (1941), *A Grammar of Motive* (1945), *A Rhetoric of Motive* (1950), *and Language as Symbolic Action* (1966).

OSCAR JAMES CAMPBELL, Professor Emeritus of English at Columbia University, has published, in addition to *Shakespeare's Satire, Comicall Satyre in Shakespeare's "Troilus and Cressida"* (1938) and *The Reader's Encyclopedia of Shakespeare* (1966).

MAURICE CHARNEY is Professor of English at Rutgers University and author of *Shakespeare's Roman Plays: The Function of Imagery in Drama* (1961).

T. S. ELIOT, the distinguished poet, playwright, and critic, wrote frequently on Shakespeare; his most important critical comments on the plays appear in his *Selected Essays* (1950).

WILLARD FARNHAM is Professor Emeritus of English at the University of California, Berkeley. In addition to *Shakespeare's Tragic Frontier*, he has published *The Medieval Heritage of Elizabethan Tragedy* (1936), and numerous articles on Shakespeare and the drama.

HARLEY GRANVILLE-BARKER, actor, playwright, director, and critic who died in 1946 is best known for his *Prefaces to Shakespeare,* an influential analysis of many of the plays in theatrical terms.

CHARLES K. HOFLING is Professor of Psychiatry at the University of Cincinnati and, in addition to numerous technical articles, the author of "Hemingway's *Old Man and the Sea* and the Male Reader" (*American Imago,* 1963).

PAUL A. JORGENSEN is Professor of English at the University of California, Los Angeles, and author of such historical and critical studies as *Shakespeare's Military World* (1956), *Redeeming Shakespeare's Words* (1962), and *Lear's Self-Discovery* (1967).

G. WILSON KNIGHT is Professor Emeritus of English at Leeds University. His interpretative studies of Shakespeare, based on close analysis of the imagery, include *The Wheel of Fire* (1930), *The Imperial Theme* (1931), *The Crown of Life* (1947), and *The Sovereign Flower* (1958).

JOHN MIDDLETON MURRY, literary critic, was editor of *The Athenaeum* and of *Adelphi* and author of such studies as *Keats and Shakespeare* (1925), *Countries of the Mind* (1922; 1931), and *Shakespeare* (1936).

JOHN PALMER succeeded Shaw and Beerbohm as dramatic critic of the *Saturday Review* until his death in 1944. He was the author of books on Restoration comedy, Ben Jonson, Molière, and the modern French theater.

RUFUS PUTNEY was, until his death in 1966, Professor of English at the University of Colorado. He published numerous articles on Shakespeare, Renaissance drama, and eighteenth-century literature. At the time of his death, he was completing a book-length study entitled *Shakespeare and the Psychiatrists*.

A. P. ROSSITER was, until his death in 1957, Lecturer at Durham and at Cambridge. In addition to *Angel with Horns*, his critical works include *English Drama* (1950).

A. A. SMIRNOV was a distinguished academic critic in the U.S.S.R. whose books and articles were among the first to discuss western European literature from the Marxist point of view.

DONALD A. STAUFFER was, before his death in 1952, Professor of English and Chairman of the Department at Princeton University. His numerous critical and historical studies range widely over the field of literature in English.

BRENTS STIRLING is Professor of English at the University of Washington. In addition to *The Populace in Shakespeare* and numerous articles, he has published books on *Unity in Shakespearian Tragedy* (1966) and *The Order of Shakespeare's Sonnets* (1968).

DEREK TRAVERSI is a critic best known for his close analyses of images and themes in Shakespeare, including *An Approach to Shakespeare* (1938) and *Shakespeare: The Last Phase* (1954).

EUGENE M. WAITH is Professor of English at Yale University and author of numerous books and articles on English drama, including *The Pattern of Tragicomedy in Beaumont and Fletcher* (1952).

Selected Bibliography

Bradley, A. C., *"Coriolanus,"* British Academy Lecture (1912), reprinted in *Studies in Shakespeare,* ed. Peter Alexander (Oxford, 1964), pp. 219–37. A classic essay on the tone of the tragedy and the moral problem of its hero.

Bullough, Geoffrey, ed., *Narrative and Dramatic Sources of Shakespeare,* Vol. V: "The Roman Plays" (London and New York, 1964), Ch. 3, pp. 453–564. A reprinting of sources and analogues with a summary of their relation to Shakespeare's play.

Goddard, Harold C., *The Meaning of Shakespeare* (Chicago, 1951; reprinted 1966), Ch. xxxii: *"Coriolanus."* A general reading of the play with emphasis on the psychoanalytical approach.

Gordon, D. J., "Name and Fame: Shakespeare's *Coriolanus,*" *Papers Mainly Shakespearian,* ed. G. I. Duthie, University of Aberdeen Studies 147 (Edinburgh, 1964), pp. 40–57. Examines Coriolanus's attitudes in the light of Renaissance ideas of personal honor and public fame.

Holland, Norman N., *Psychoanalysis and Shakespeare* (New York, 1966), pp. 157–62 and 328–29. A full and judicious survey of current psychoanalytical interpretations of the play.

MacCullum, M. W., *Shakespeare's Roman Plays and Their Background* (London, 1952), Ch. II: *"Coriolanus."* The first, and still authoritative, general account of the tragedy in relation to its sources, circumstances, and significance as a Roman play.

Phillips, James E., *The State in Shakespeare's Greek and Roman Plays* (New York, 1940), Ch. VIII: "Violation of Order and Degree in *Coriolanus.*" An examination of the ways in which the play employs Renaissance concepts of the nature of political society.

Ribner, Irving, *Patterns in Shakespearian Tragedy* (New York, 1960), pp. 184–201. A perceptive thematic analysis of the central paradox presented in the play.

Richmond, H. M., *Shakespeare's Political Plays* (New York, 1967), Part IV, Ch. 2: *"Coriolanus."* A scholarly study of the play as a confrontation between a virtuous superman and political reality.

Zeeveld, W. Gordon, "*Coriolanus* and Jacobean Politics." *Modern Language Review* LVII (1962), 321–34. A discussion of the play in the light of contemporary Parliamentary movements for popular government.

TWENTIETH CENTURY
INTERPRETATIONS

MAYNARD MACK, *Series Editor*
Yale University

NOW AVAILABLE
Collections of Critical Essays
ON

(continued on next page)

(continued from previous page)

MAJOR BARBARA
MEASURE FOR MEASURE
THE MERCHANT OF VENICE
MOLL FLANDERS
MUCH ADO ABOUT NOTHING
THE NIGGER OF THE "NARCISSUS"
OEDIPUS REX
THE OLD MAN AND THE SEA
PAMELA
THE PLAYBOY OF THE WESTERN WORLD
THE PORTRAIT OF A LADY
A PORTRAIT OF THE ARTIST AS A YOUNG MAN
THE PRAISE OF FOLLY
PRIDE AND PREJUDICE
THE RAPE OF THE LOCK
THE RIME OF THE ANCIENT MARINER
ROBINSON CRUSOE
ROMEO AND JULIET
SAMSON AGONISTES
THE SCARLET LETTER
SIR GAWAIN AND THE GREEN KNIGHT
SONGS OF INNOCENCE AND OF EXPERIENCE
SONS AND LOVERS
THE SOUND AND THE FURY
THE TEMPEST
TESS OF THE D'URBERVILLES
TOM JONES
TWELFTH NIGHT
UTOPIA
VANITY FAIR
WALDEN
THE WASTE LAND
WOMEN IN LOVE
WUTHERING HEIGHTS